Psychological Machinery

Dalibor Vobořil / Petr Květon /
Martin Jelínek

Psychological Machinery

Experimental Devices in Early
Psychological Laboratories

Bibliographic Information published by the Deutsche Nationalbibliothek
The Deutsche Nationalbibliothek lists this publication
in the Deutsche Nationalbibliografie; detailed bibliographic
data is available in the internet at http://dnb.d-nb.de.

Library of Congress Cataloging-in-Publication Data
Voboril, Dalibor, 1973–
 [Experimentální přístrojová technika v raných psychologických laboratořích. English]
 Psychological machinery : experimental devices in early psychological laboratories / Dalibor Voboril, Petr Kveton, Martin Jelínek.
   pages cm
 Includes bibliographical references and index.
 ISBN 978-3-631-64130-9
 1. Psychological apparatus. 2. Psychology, Experimental. I. Kveton, Petr, 1975– II. Jelínek, Martin, 1978– III. Title.
 BF80.V6313 2014
 150.28'4—dc23
                                                     2013047473

Cover image: © 2013 Dalibor Voboril,
The Fall Tachistoscope

ISBN 978-3-631-64130-9 (Print)
E-ISBN 978-3-653-03082-2 (E-Book)
DOI 10.3726/978-3-653-03082-2
© Peter Lang GmbH
Internationaler Verlag der Wissenschaften
Frankfurt am Main 2014
All rights reserved.
PKL Academic Research is an Imprint of Peter Lang GmbH.

Peter Lang – Frankfurt am Main · Bern · Bruxelles · New York ·
Oxford · Warszawa · Wien

All parts of this publication are protected by copyright. Any
utilisation outside the strict limits of the copyright law, without
the permission of the publisher, is forbidden and liable to
prosecution. This applies in particular to reproductions,
translations, microfilming, and storage and processing in
electronic retrieval systems.

www.peterlang.com

Preface

The book you are holding aims to provide information on one of the unjustly neglected areas of experimental psychology. Founding fathers of the experimental tradition in psychology left behind an invaluable body of work, knowledge, ideas and concepts described in books or noted down in experimental notebooks. This enduring legacy of thought, which serves as a basis for most modern theories, is supplemented by a whole range of extant unique instruments. It is these remarkable experimental devices that represent the neglected domain we are referring to. Our book attempts to provide at least a partial remedy for the situation by addressing this fascinating aspect of the scientific psychological past in detail.

When preparing the contents of this book, we had to bury ourselves in the original sources to find scattered mentions of specific instruments and technical refinements needed for their proper operation. Our journey against the tide of time led through a pathway edged with books and journals of publication dates starting with 18-, written in archaic language that was not always easy to understand. Still, the magic of tiny unexpected revelations provided us with enough drive and energy to walk the way, and our endeavor was rewarded with an intriguing glimpse into the realm of technical instrumentation used in the original experimental studies, dating back to the times when psychology as a scientific discipline was formed.

To be able to grasp and adequately describe each particular piece of equipment, we had to put on lab coats and get our hands dirty with dust and grime university collections had been gathering for decades. This way we could improve our often scanty literature-based knowledge through practical experience.

In the book, we decided to focus on detailed description of the individual experimental instruments. Considering the large number of devices covered, we had to reduce our ambitions of including details on their specific use in experimental studies. On top of that, such attempts might have been misleading anyway since the purpose of most instruments was generic, and the equipment could be used in many different designs depending on the creative approach of the experimenter. Instead, we chose to describe the instruments in a very detailed manner that encourages the readers to infer all possible ways of application on their own.

It is better to see once than to read a hundred times...
Bearing in mind this proverbial saying, we supplemented selected instrument descriptions with QR codes linked to web-pages which contain videos showing how the instruments operate. We hope that readers will enjoy the encounter with equipment designed and used by the founding fathers of experimental psychology as much as we did.

Acknowledgments

We would like to thank all people and institutions that contributed to the monograph. Namely, we would like to thank Professor Henning Schmidgen and the entire *Virtual Laboratory* project (http://vlp.mpiwg-berlin.mpg.de) for access to a large collection of original works. Furthermore, we thank Dr. A. Meischner-Metge from the University of Leipzig for clarifying the details of Wundt's laboratory and for a pair of original images of laboratory interior. Likewise, we would like to express our gratitude to Rand B. Evans, Professor Emeritus of Psychology at East Carolina University and (deceased) Jiří Hoskovec, Emeritus Professor at Charles University in Prague for the materials and valuable advice. Last but not least, we would like to thank the Institute of Psychology of Faculty of Arts of Masaryk University for the opportunity to work with the collection of original experimental devices. Study was supported by RVO: 68081740.

Table of Contents

Introduction 1
The Origins of Psychological Laboratories 2
    Wundt's Laboratory: A Closer Look 5
    Psychological Laboratories around the World 9
Methodology of Working with Historical Sources - Putting Pieces Together 10
    The Cost of Experimental Research 12
Experimental Equipment at the Turn of the 20th Century 14
    Instruments with Time-Related Functions 15
        Time Measuring and Recording Devices 15
        Calibration Devices for Chronoscopes 21
        Impulse Generating Devices 22
        Reaction Keys 28
        Tuning Forks 33
    Recording Devices 37
        Kymographs 37
        Kymograph Accessories 44
        Registration Devices 47
    Devices for Research of Visual Perception 56
        Color Mixing Devices 56
        Episcotisters 62
        Tachistoscopes 63
        Perimeters 70
        Other Equipment 73
    Devices for Research of Tactual Perception 75
    Instruments Used for Study of Hearing 80
        Hammering Devices 80
        Wind Instruments 83
        Accessories for Auditory Perception Devices 88

Devices for Research of Olfaction and Taste 90
Devices for Research of Memory and Learning 91
Instruments for the Measurement of Physiological Variables 95
    Cardiographs 95
    Pneumographs 97
    Plethysmographs 100
    Manometers 101
    Sphygmographs 102
Devices for Measurement of Muscle Characteristics 105
    Tremometers 105
    Ergographs 106
    Dynamometers 108
Other Tools and Devices 109
Auxiliary Devices 113
    Switches 113
    Response Curve Measuring Devices 114
    Batteries and Accumulators 116
    Transmissions, Engines and Tachometers 118

Conclusion 120
Summary 121
Bibliography 122
Instrument Index 128

Introduction

After centuries of polemic disputations about how body and mind are related, what the role human consciousness is, or how human soul can be healed, the acceptance of scientific methods moved psychology closer to evidence-based natural sciences. The inception of scientific psychology with its experimental devices and instruments at the end of the 19th century can be considered as the first step towards the establishment of a well-organized and critical research of human mind. Wilhelm Wundt himself noted that psychological introspection should come hand in hand with methods of experimental physiology. The application of these methods on psychological introspection would lead to the psychophysical method as an independent discipline in the field of experimental research.

At the end of the 19th century, the highly advanced discipline of physiology contributed to the birth of modern scientific psychology by providing elaborated experimental instruments and devices. First psychological laboratories were established, and the researchers gradually adapted the physiological instruments to their own needs, or started to design their own instruments according to specific research goals.

In this book we focus primarily on that part of psychological history, which is not – despite its considerable significance – completely covered in the relevant literature. More specifically, we will describe experimental instruments and devices used in psychological research at the turn of the 20th century. The book was inspired by the unique collections of historical apparatus kept on the premises of Masaryk University in Brno and Charles University in Prague, as well as the collection maintained by Technical Museum in Brno. These collections comprise a set of instruments which represent typical experimental equipment found in any respectable university laboratory in Europe of that time. Our efforts focused on identification, classification and description of mechanical design of most relevant instrumental equipment. Technical details are supplemented with the description of each instrument's purpose and operation. In some cases we also tried to map the process in which experimental psychologists used their ingenuity in incorporating contemporary advances in technology into the construction of even more sophisticated devices. These advancements illustrate the progressivity of psychology as an independent scientific field which is able to absorb new pieces of information from different areas of science and engineering and integrate them into its own methodological base.

2
The Origins of Psychological Laboratories

At the very beginning, psychology was driven by joint efforts of scientists from various fields, such as physiology, philosophy, or biology (Harper, 1950). These fields shared a common object of interest, but they examined it with different methods and from different perspectives. Continual cooperation between the researchers combined with ceaseless sharing of ideas eventually led to the establishment of experimental psychology as a separate scientific discipline. The viability of the new field was proven with the founding of the first psychological laboratories in the last quarter of the 19th century. The work environment and instrumental equipment of psychological laboratories predetermined research interests and opportunities in such a way, that the laboratory as a whole could be viewed as a universal research tool.

The laboratory of Prof. Wilhelm Maxmilian Wundt (16 August 1832 – 31 August 1920) is considered the first psychological experimental facility. The laboratory was established at the Leipzig University[1], thus securing the university a prominent position in the history of psychology. It served as a gold standard for all latter laboratories spread around the world, as mentioned by McK. Cattell in 1888 (p. 39): "It is interesting to note that the example set by Wundt at Leipsic is being followed in other universities. Psychological laboratories have been established or are being planned at Berlin, Bonn, Göttingen; in America, at Johns Hopkins, Harvard, Pennsylvania and Princeton; in England at Cambridge; also at Copenhagen and elsewhere." The Leipzig Institute – as Wundt used to refer to his own laboratory – was also an important centre of development of new instruments. Experimental work on verifying postulated theories often required construction of new prototypes able to measure the target characteristics or adaptation of instruments known from the field of experimental physiology. Wilhelm Wundt made good use of his university education in medicine and physiology, as well as of his internship with Hermann von Helmholtz and collaboration with physiologists Johannes Müller and Emil du Bois-Reymond.

Wundt's interest in experimental work naturally anteceded the moment of founding his well-known laboratory, which is illustrated in the diary of Czech philosopher Josef Dastich. This scholar travelled across Europe and visited famous scientists, among others also Helmholtz and, in 1865, Wundt in Heidelberg (Lifka, 1923): "… Then I had been looking for Prof. Wundt for a long time, even though he lived on the main street across from the Institute; I did not ask, rely-

---

[1] The Leipzig University was established in 1409 by German teachers and students who left Prague during the reign of King Wenceslaus IV (Otto, 1900, p. 83). The structure of Leipzig University therefore resembles the organization of Charles University in Prague.

ing on 'Personalstand' – in fact he moved to a new apartment in the 'zum Riesen' house. He lives with his parents – judicial councilor – he has a very kind mother; he welcomed me very warmly. We discussed local conditions and I am grateful for many advices. The next week he will start a new, for me personally interesting, series of lectures 'Anthrop'. He reads in his apartment and willingly offered me, almost before I asked him, to come and see, if I could make use of any of it. Also to visit his instrument collections and perform some experimental trials together. Naturally, I'll be glad to do both..."

Wundt's laboratory grew up from very humble beginnings. After a year spent at the University of Zurich, in May 1875 Wundt received a letter from Friedrich Zarnde from Leipzig with an offer of a 'modest position' at the university. This position represented only a half of what was originally a single professorial post, and the other half was offered to Max Heinz from Königsberg. After a brief consideration Wundt accepted and in the very same month (October 1875) was appointed a regular professor of philosophy. In addition to that, the Royal Ministry with the agreement of the academic senate assigned him several rooms in the university Konvikt building (Wundt, 1920). Wundt used these rooms as storage space for his experimental instruments and teaching requisites. In 1879 he founded his own private institute which only occupied four rooms where students started doing experimental work under his supervision. Therefore, 1879 is recognized as the year of the first psychological laboratory foundation (Boring, 1950).

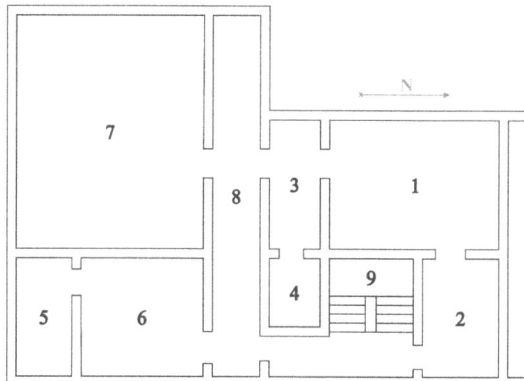

Figure 1. The layout of Wundt's laboratory in Konvikt (Hoskovec, Nakonečný, Sedláková, 2003). Detailed description is provided in the text.

Among the first students of Wundt's institute one can find famous names like G. Stanley Hall and Max Friedrich. We can hypothesize that these two psychologists were most likely the first experimenters as there are records from data collection for Friedrich's thesis (On the Duration of Apperception of Complex Images) conducted in December 1879, which in 1881 also became the first doctoral thesis defended at the Institute (Benjamin, 1997). Since 1879 Wundt's laboratory provided courses and workshops, even though they were not listed in the official university study programs. Only in the summer semester 1881 Wundt's laboratory classes was first introduced to the study program. Some of the most notable students in these early years included Emil Kraepelin, G. Stanley Hall, and Wundt's future assistant James McKeen Cattell.

Another significant year was 1883 when the Royal Ministry officially approved funding for the Private Institute, and on June 26 the Institute became a part of the university as the 26th department called the Institute for Experimental Psychology. Soon after that, the university advertised for the post of an assistant at the Institute and the Seminar on Experimental Psychology could appear in the university study program (Wundt, 1909). At the same time, the Institute was assigned two additional rooms formerly used by the Institute of Pharmacology. Figure 1 depicts the new layout of the Institute (Benjamin, 1997) – lecture rooms (1 and 7), conference room (2), waiting room (3), darkroom (4), laboratories (5 and 6), and hallway (8) with staircase (9). The rooms were newly equipped with gas fixtures for proper lighting and electricity for instruments requiring higher voltage than voltage provided by batteries (Benjamin, 1997). A subjective review of the Institute was provided by Krohn (1892), who considered some of the instruments obsolete and deserving replacement, usable mainly for demonstration and educational purposes. He also remarked that the laboratory rooms were equipped with good lighting, but very bad quality floors. On the other hand, Krohn also made a reference to the sophisticated Ludwig-Baltazar's kymograph, which was only owned by two laboratories at that time – Wundt's laboratory in Leipzig and the laboratory in Bonn. At the institute Krohn also mentioned meeting with August Kirschmann (later a director of the Psychological Laboratory at the University of Toronto) and Oswald Külpe (founder of the laboratory in Würtzburg).

In the early years the Institute engaged in various research activities. Cattel (1888) classified the research interests into four areas: (1) Analysis and Measurement of Sensation; (2) Duration of Mental Processes; (3) Time-Sense; and (4) Attention, Memory and Association of Ideas. In 1883 the Institute undertook in total 19 research projects with worldwide student participation, comprising Americans, Russians, Scandinavians, Czechs, Greeks, and Frenchmen. The publication of the journal Philosophischen Studien was launched in the same year. The contents of the journal were primarily devoted to the laboratory's research methods and findings.

Starting in 1890, the university experienced considerable growth, which also significantly influenced Wundt's laboratory. In connection with a complex reconstruction of the university, the Konvikt building was torn down, and the Institute was temporarily moved to the Triersche Institut on the Grimmaischen Steinweg Street. At the Triersche Institut Wundt's laboratory found its place on the second floor of the Grimm Haus on Steinweg 12, Leipzig, where it occupied eleven offices. This increment in space enabled further expansion of the laboratory by means of admitting more students and extending its research activities. In summer 1894 another assistant position was approved and the daily work routine of the laboratory settled to the period from 2 p.m. till 7 p.m. Monday to Friday and from 2 p.m. till 4 p.m. on Saturday. In autumn 1896, as soon as the reconstruction of the university was finished, the Institute moved again, this time settling in the upper floor of the two connected buildings Johanneum and Paulinum (see Figure 2).

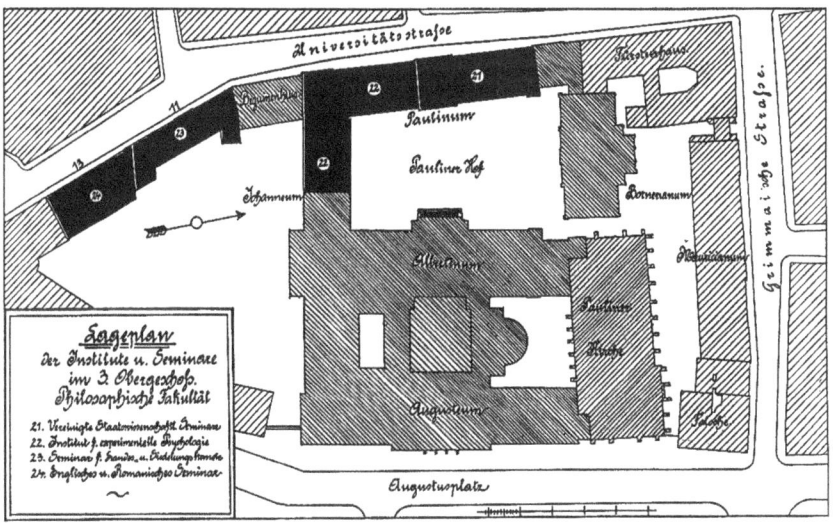

Figure 2. The location of Wundt's laboratory at the Faculty of Arts, Leipzig University (Wundt, 1909). Mark 22 – Institute of Experimental Psychology.

Wundt's Laboratory: A Closer Look

To summarize, Wundt's laboratory was successively situated in three different locations. Originally established in the Konvikt building (1874-~1890), the laboratory temporarily moved to the Grimm Haus (~1890-1896) during the university's reconstruction, and then in 1896 it was settled in the university buildings Johanneum and Paulinum until 1943 when these buildings were bombed out to the ground.

Since Wundt's Institute for Experimental Psychology in Johanneum and Paulinum was designed on the basis of long-term experience with experimental work, its layout and workflow patterns became a standard for other laboratories scattered around the world. Detailed description of the Institute can be found in Wundt's (1909) article The Institute for Experimental Psychology, which was included in the proceedings published on the occasion of the 500th anniversary of the Leipzig University.

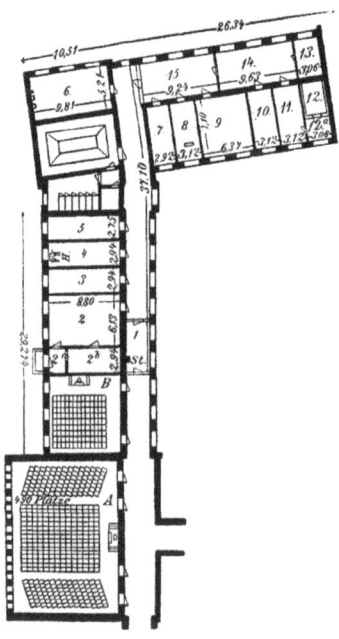

Figure 3. The layout of Wundt's laboratory in Johanneum and Paulinum (Wundt, 1909). Detailed description provided in the text.

The largest room of the Institute was the auditorium (letter A in Figure 3) for 490 students. This vast capacity was needed because psychology belonged to the compulsory courses at the faculty. The auditorium was amphitheatric with regularly shaped tall windows and atrium lighting. Black curtains pulled by electric motors enabled partial darkening. The lecturer's desk was equipped with electrical cabling and gas fixtures. Moreover, it was connected to the instruments in the laboratory rooms via cable wiring. The neighboring lecture hall (letter B) with the same equipment only provided 98 seats and enabled complete darkening.

There were two entrances to the Institute – one from the Albertinum building (see Figure 2) across the room marked with no. 1 in Figure 3, and the other through the staircase between rooms 5 and 6. Room 2 was used for optical experiments and was equipped with darkening black curtains (as well as rooms 5 and 11). The room was partitioned, with sections 2a and 2b, painted matt black, serving as dark rooms. Heliostats for experiments with natural sunlight were installed on the balcony, which was south oriented. Section 2a served as a storage space for an arc lamp with accessories and a charging station for accumulators (the charging process produced toxic gas which had to be cleared from the room). Office 3 was occupied by the head of the Institute[2].

Illustrational teaching tools were stored in corner room 6, which was also used for Institute staff meetings. There were also 60 Meidinger's cells kept in this room, which provided stable direct current for some instruments such as chronoscopes. Capacity sources in room 6 were connected with all other rooms through heavy current wiring. In cases when stable current was not necessary, standard 110 V university wiring was used. All laboratory rooms in the Institute were also interconnected by telephone (data) lines.

The Paulinum wing was oriented in the direction from east to west. Room 15 served as a changing room and a storage space for demonstration boards used in lectures. Library and reading space were set in room 14. At the far end of the wing there was a workroom (13) equipped for the maintenance of mechanical instruments. Rooms 7 – 12 were separated by a massive wall from the other rooms and had double-pane windows oriented to the university's inner yard. These rooms were specifically designated for experiments with acoustic stimuli. Room 8 also had linoleum flooring to reduce footstep noise. Rooms 9 and 12 were even made almost totally soundproof using sandwich walls and upholstered doors. An enclosed subdivision of room 12, with no windows and walls painted black, could serve as a soundproof dark room.

Department of Psychology at the Leipzig University was kind enough to provide us with two photographs allowing us a look into the inner space of the Institute. Unfortunately, since these photos are undated, we can only hypothesize in which of the three locations they were taken. However, there are several clues in the pictures that can help us specify the time period. As we know, gas fixtures were installed in the Konvikt building during its reconstruction in 1883, and gas pipes and lamps are clearly visible in the right photograph in Figure 4. We also know that in the third location there were electrical wiring and lighting installed in the laboratory (after 1896), which are not present in the pictures. These clues strongly suggest that the photographs capture the appearance of the Institute in its second location between 1883 and 1896. The configuration of the depicted instruments also supports this conclusion.

---

2   Chronologically: Wilhelm Wundt (1896-1917), Felix Krüeger (1917-1936), Phillip Lersch (1939-1943).

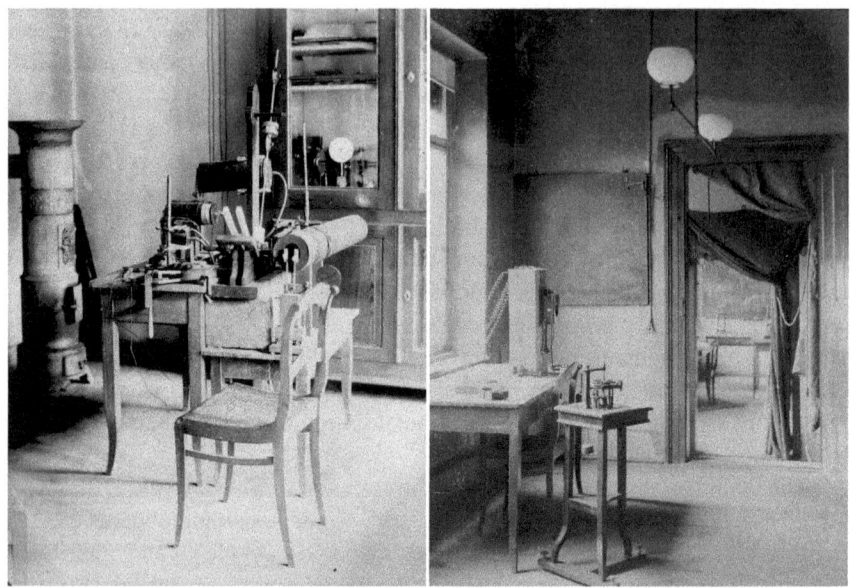

Figure 4.   Photographs of Wundt's laboratory rooms (the Leipzig University archive)

In the early years of the Institute's existence the necessary technical equipment was provided by mechanic Karl Krille. After his death the role of the main supplier of mechanical instruments was passed to Ernst Zimmermann. Many of the instruments were designed by Wundt himself or by other researchers in the laboratory, and it was Zimmermann who was particularly able to turn their ideas into the form of actual original instruments (Wundt, 1909). Zimmermann the Mechanic started his company in 1887 in Leipzig (Gundlach, 1983). Shortly after, he established a partnership with Psychological Institute at Leipzig University, which significantly stimulated the company's growth. Many students from around the world got in touch with Zimmermann's instruments at Wundt's Institute and after returning back home they ordered them for their own laboratories. This way Zimmermann multiplied his sales, and, consequently, the original custom production for Leipzig Institute was upgraded to mass production. Methodologically speaking, this virtual monopoly on the supply of research instruments led to considerable standardization of measurement and to the possibility of experiment replication and comparison of results yielded by different research facilities across the world.

Psychological Laboratories around the World

Approximately at the same time when Wundt officially started his experimental work in the Konvikt building, another giant of those days, William James, established a laboratory at the Harvard University in the United States. There is still some controversy regarding the primacy of Wundt versus James in founding the world's first experimental laboratory (Harper, 1950). However, more than the actual controversy what we find particularly relevant is the principal goal which each laboratory was founded for. While Wundt had strong drive to perform experimental research in a rigorous way, James was more philosophically oriented and used the laboratory mainly for educational purposes. James felt relieved when he handed the laboratory over to Hugo Münsterberg, Wundt's former graduate student and research assistant (Bjork, 1983). Wundt's tremendous impact on the growth of experimental psychology worldwide is also well documented by the number of students who followed in his footsteps and founded their own laboratories in other cities and countries. There were fourteen laboratories founded by eleven students of Wundt (10 laboratories in the US, 3 in Germany and 1 in Denmark and 1 in Canada) as contrasted with three laboratories founded by James' students (all in the US). Several laboratories could theoretically be assigned to both lines because they were founded by students of G. Stanley Hall who studied both at Wundt's and James' institutes (for more details see Figure 5).

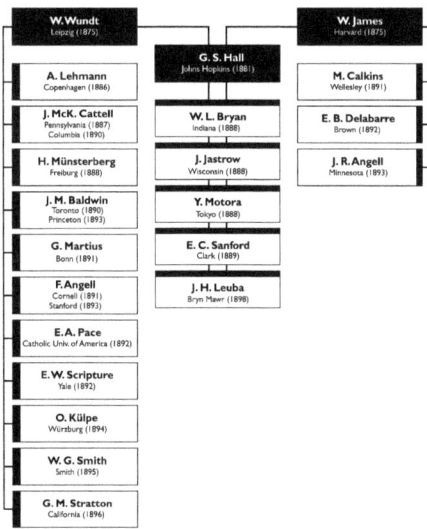

Figure 5.   *Timeline of the establishment of psychological laboratories by Wundt's and James' students (Harper, 1950)*

Methodology of Working with Historical Sources - Putting Pieces Together

When working with original instruments from the turn of the 20th century, the ultimate sources of information one can refer to are E. Zimmermann's catalogue from 1903 and Spindler & Hoyer's catalogue from 1921. Besides these two famous catalogues we also drew on other historical sources, such as Methodology of Physiological Experiments and Vivisection by Cyon (1876b), or Langendorff's (1891) guide to physiological graphical recording methods. The bank of knowledge accumulated from all these sources helped us identify and classify the instruments and accurately describe their functionality. In several cases we were even able to locate and identify individual components of dismantled instruments and put all parts together into complete devices.

For experimental studies published at the beginning of the 20th century it was not necessary to provide a detailed description of the functionality of every single piece of equipment used, since most scientists of that time were familiar with these instruments. The problem is that today's researchers studying such original papers have virtually no means of accessing this knowledge. A great deal of historical equipment has been lost and forgotten, and its functionality is currently unknown or might have been misinterpreted. For example, when reading an article by of one of the founders of modern Czech psychology Vilém Chmelař published in 1935 in the authoritative journal Psychology, the reader finds no less than three different instruments mentioned in a single sentence: "Graphical autoregistration by Römer's acoustic key connected to electromagnetic marker and Jaquet's chronograph was replaced..." (Chmelař, 1935, p. 32). Can you decide which of the drawings in Figure 6 depicts Römer's acoustic key?

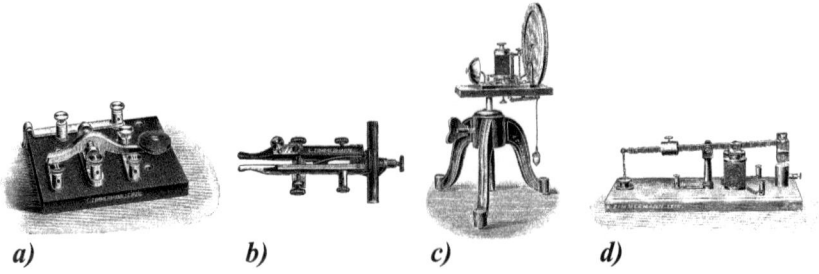

a) *b)* *c)* *d)*

Figure 6.   Which of the instruments is Römer's acoustic key?

This brief example illustrates the difficulty of assigning a label to a particular instrument (you got the right answer if you chose option c), as you can check on page 31 of this boook). This is the reason why curators of scientific museums managed by prestigious universities often have to deal with the problem of 'mystery' instruments, i.e. the presence of unrecognized scientific artifacts in the collection. The collection kept at the premises of Masaryk University originally contained several unidentified instruments. One case that is especially worth mentioning is the Case of a Mystery Box: Having found a small black box with three strange-looking shiny metal tubes inside, we had absolutely no clue and no one to ask what it actually was and what function it used to serve. It required almost detective skill, looking through thousands of old dusty pages, hoping to find a match. In the end, however, we successfully cracked the case and could ceremonially place the box on a shelf with a small label reading "Politzer's Acoumeter" (see Figure 7, more on page 81).

Figure 7.   Politzer's Acoumeter – The case of a mystery box

The Cost of Experimental Research

Most experimental work nowadays is carried out by computerized equipment. Almost every student today owns a personal computer which can (with the appropriate software installed) serve as a small experimental laboratory. However, at the beginning of the 20th century the only way to achieve precision in experimental measurement was by means of mechanic, pneumatic, or simple electric devices.

Designing and manufacturing such devices was not an easy task, which is also why the costs were considerably high. It is understandable that it was mainly specialized university laboratories who bought instrument collections. Still, some students were enthusiastic enough to use their own financial resources to purchase a private set of instruments. Such wealthy and enthusiastic students once were also later professors Wundt (1909), Titchener (1895), or McK. Cattell (1928).

Even Zimmermann's catalogue from 1902 (on page 2) targeted students in its marketing communication: "The design [of a single kymograph] is elegant and solid, so that it can contribute to the decoration of every laboratory, medical room or student's room." This 'decoration' (see Figure 8) in basic configuration was worth 175 marks. With all additional accessories (sensors, connection components, etc.), the price added up to 375 marks.

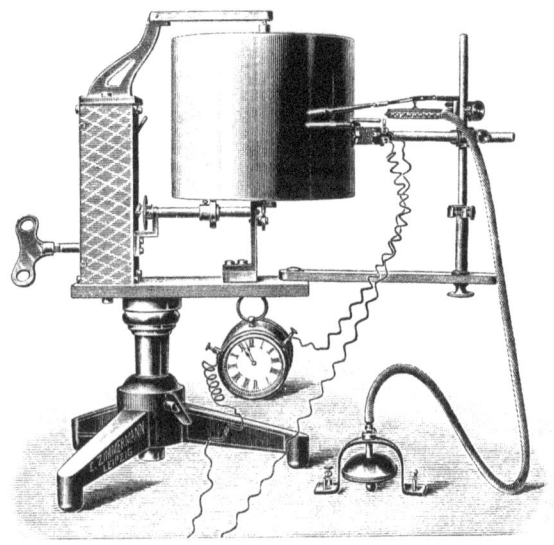

Figure 8. A simple kymograph (Zimmermann, 1909)

To obtain a proper picture of the financial context of the period in question, we may, for example, refer to the public speech given in Hannover by the social democrat August Bebel (Klein, 1977, p. 81) in 1899: "... the average yearly family income is lower than 900 marks. The average yearly salary of a German worker is about 600 – 700 marks. Saxon and Silesian weavers are eking out their existence with 300 – 400 marks a year..." The speech continued in the same emotional vein, mentioning only few facts, including average annual expenses on shoes and clothing for a family, amounting to 20 – 40 marks. Financial demands connected with acquiring scientific instruments can also be assessed by comparing their prices to the price of one metric ton of black coal, which was approximately 13 marks (Klein, 1977).

Setting up and maintaining a laboratory required considerable investments. The annual budget of Wundt's laboratory in the time directly following its establishment in 1879 fluctuated between 600 and 900 marks; twenty years later, it rose to 2000 marks per year (Wundt, 1909). When looking at the pricelist in Zimmermann's catalogue from today's perspective, we might consider this budget as rather low. For example, a set of devices for stimulus presentation and time measurement needed in a simple word-association experiment (even without a recording device) was worth 782 marks.

A similar view of the issue of financing necessary laboratory equipment was expressed by prof. Gundlach (1983) in his note on the back of Zimmermann's catalogue reprint's cover: "Zimmermann's pricelists and catalogues include an almost complete technological palette of instruments which comprised psychological laboratory equipment of that time, while nearly none of the institutes was so well-situated as to be able to afford all of the instruments advertised in the catalogue." Not much has changed since Wundt's time with regard to the matter of funding laboratory equipment.

Experimental Equipment at the Turn of the 20th Century

This central part of the book provides an account of experimental apparatus used in psychological laboratories around the time between 1880 and 1930. In some cases, however, we delved even deeper into the history and attempted to describe the original experimental tools of early physiological laboratories, which served as prototypes for instruments adjusted for the needs of experimental psychology.

Although the book introduces a considerably large number of instruments, this number surely does not include all possibilities of obtaining experimental data at that time. Still, we believe that all principal solutions are at least broadly outlined by the descriptions provided, as the book covers almost the entire collection of original experimental equipment housed by the Psychology Department of Masaryk University and the Technical Museum in Brno, dating from the period in question.

The technical terms used to describe various instruments in different languages (German and English) were taken from the Zimmermann catalogue, as we assumed that the terminology contained in the catalogue was idiomatic and most commonly used at the time of publication (1928). We found no significant divergences when checking other sources for instrument names (e.g. the Spindler and Hoyer catalogues from 1908 and 1921 respectively). We also preserved the original spelling of the foreign language expressions used in the late 19th and early 20th century. This way, the terminology is consistent with references in scientific literature of that time, which should make working with original sources easier for the reader.

The instruments are grouped in the individual chapters according to their specialized functions and applications. In some cases it was rather difficult to decide in which chapter a particular instrument would fit best, since the device or tool could as well be used in another type of experiment which might not have been directly related to its primary purpose. One example of such a tool is the tuning fork which, after some thought on our part, was not placed among acoustic instruments but was included in the chapter on the measurement and manipulation of time-related variables.

While the book principally describes laboratory instruments designed in the workshop of E. Zimmermann, it must be noted that Zimmermann's factory was not nearly the only co-designer and manufacturer of such equipment at that time. In fact, one could provide a whole list of technicians and companies specializing in scientific equipment in the early days of psychology and physiology. Among the most prominent names we might mention Gerhard Baltzar, who collaborated with physiologist Carl Ludwig on the original design of kymograph (Cyon, 1876b), K. Krille, the co-designer of what later came to be known as the Wundt Chronograph (Wundt, 1909), or Rudolph Koenig, the then top manufacturer of acoustic devices (Boring, 1942) and a close associate of Hermann von Helmholtz. A humble illustration of how far the list might go is provided by the equipment inventory of the psychological laboratory at the University of Groningen, established in 1892 by Gerard Heymans. The total number of 67 instruments came from 18 suppliers. In most cases, each manufacturer provided one or two pieces, with the exception of E. Zimmermann, who supplied 22 devices. Eight instruments were designed directly in the laboratory, and for 17 pieces the supplier was not stated (Draaisma, 1992). Similarly, Hugo Münsterberg, (1893) whose Harvard University laboratory inventory contained as much as 240 items, listed 67 manufacturers, 54 of which were European, and the rest were American.

In the region of today's Czech Republic, a notable workshop was run by Rudolf Rothe, a university mechanic of the German Institute of Physiology, who worked in collaboration with Ewald Hering[3]. Around 1895, however, both Rothe and Hering left Prague, and Rothe moved his factory to Leipzig[4]. Another reference of this kind involves Dr. Pleskot Company mentioned in an article describing Krejčí's tachistoscope variant, published in the journal Česká mysl (Rameš, 1928).

Instruments with Time-Related Functions

The first category of instruments to be addressed comprises tools and devices measuring and/or manipulating one of the most important variables in experimental psychology – time. The following chapter describes different ways and options for measuring and recording reaction time, calibration equipment for timing devices, means of obtaining control time pulses for stimulus generators, as well as a variety of reaction keys.

Time Measuring and Recording Devices

According to Perera and Haupt (2000), the first attempt to measure an extremely short time interval can be dated back to the year 1840. At that time the physicist Charles Wheatstone challenged the military problem of how to measure the ini-

---

3 Instruments made by Ewald Hering's design can be found in the Rothe's catalogue (1893).
4 This is documented by Rothe's correspondence with Professor Titchener found in the collection of Professor R. Evans.

tial velocity of fired artillery shells. Wheatstone (among others, the inventor of telegraph and rheostat) set up a device which closed an electric circuit at the very moment when the projectile left the muzzle of a gun and interrupted the current when the projectile hit the target. This circuit controlled a clockwork mechanism situated in a safe location. In 1842, the Swiss clock smith Mathias Hipp improved the accuracy of Wheatstone's design by incorporating a 500 Hz tuning fork which controlled the speed of cogwheel rotation.

The devices measuring short intervals of time soon proved to be very helpful in experimental psychology, allowing the researchers to collect valuable data. In 1868, Dutch ophthalmologist F. C. Donders published his study focusing on the speed of mental processes, which, until that time, were considered unmeasurable (Donders, 1868). Reaction time measurement quickly became an essential and broadly used research technique. For example, at Wundt's Institute more than 50 % of all experimental work involved the measurement of reaction times (Cattell, 1888).

Hipp's Chronoscope

Chronoskop nach Hipp (GE)

Figure 9. Chronoscope According to Hipp (Spindler & Hoyer, 1908)

Hipp's Chronoscope is a very accurate and reliable time measuring device which used to belong to the basic equipment of early laboratories. Some of its variants make it possible to measure time intervals with accuracy as high as 1/1000 sec. To ensure a perfectly even pace, the clockwork should be started a short moment prior to the actual measurement.

The core component of the machine is a vibrating (with the exact frequency of 1/1000 sec) lamella with an escape wheel. The actual time measurement is initiated by an electromagnet which pulls the clock face mechanism to the clockwork.

At the end of measurement the current is interrupted, the electromagnet stops acting on the clock face mechanism, and a spring pushes it out. The inertial motion of the dial hands is prevented by connecting the mechanism to a fixed wheel. The instrument has two dials, one indicating 1/10 sec, and the other 1/1000 sec. Vibration of the lamella produces distinctive sound which can be checked against a tuning fork (Schraven, 2004). After several trials, it is recommended to verify the accuracy of the device by means of a controlling instrument (like Hipp's Drop Apparatus or other calibration devices presented in chapter Calibration Devices for Chronoscopes).

The largest models of chronoscopes were intended for demonstration purposes in large lecture halls. They had backlit dials made of milk glass with a diameter up to 46 cm. Wundt had one of such instruments installed in the lecture room of his Institute (Wundt, 1909).

Hipp's Drop Apparatus

Fallapparat nach Hipp (GE)

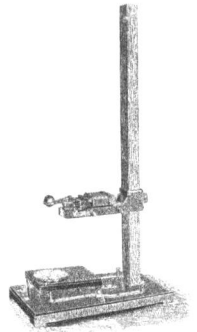

Figure 10. Hipp's Drop Apparatus (Zimmermann, 1922b)

In contrast to Hipp's chronoscope, the function of this apparatus is not time measurement but precise indication of a pre-set time interval. The main principle is based on letting a body of particular mass fall a pre-determined distance. In this case, the body is represented by a steel ball which is released from a clamp mechanism carried by a rider when the apparatus is connected to the electric circuit. When the ball hits the bottom contact surface, the circuit is interrupted. The length of the ball's fall thus determines the interval in which the current is running through the closed circuit. This way it is possible to run an external device for a predetermined time interval by connecting it to the circuit of the drop apparatus. This technique was broadly used in physiology (e.g. Cyon, 1876b). As a side-effect, the ball hitting the landing surface produced a sharp sound. While physiologists generally considered this side-effect undesirable, Wundt's student Friedrich (1883) utilized the sound as a stimulus in his reaction time experiment[5]. When the hit on the landing surface closes the electric circuit, the electric current activates a chronoscope. The circuit is interrupted, and the chronoscope stops, when the test subject responds to the sound by pressing a key. The obtained time interval represents the subject's reaction time to an acoustic signal.

To avoid the disturbing noise of the electromagnetic clamp releasing the ball from the rider, there was a variant of Hipp's Drop Apparatus without clamps. In this case, the ball was dropped manually through a ringlet (Zimmermann, 1903).

Jaquet's Graphic Chronometer[6]

Graphische Chronometer nach Jaquet (GE)

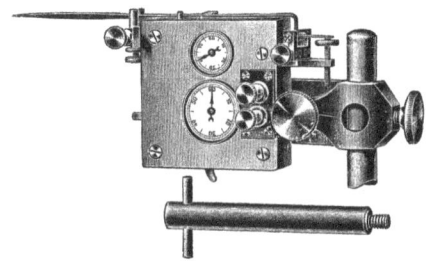

Figure 11. Jaquet's Graphic Chronometer (Zimmermann, 1922c)

The function of Jaquet's chronometer is to anchor observed events in time by means of scratching a time axis into a layer of carbon black on a recording sheet which is usually handled by a kymograph (see page 37). The time axis provides an accurate time reference for the events observed. The device contains a high precision clockwork mechanism which moves the hands of two dials. The larger bottom dial shows minutes whereas the smaller one on the top shows seconds[7]. The time axis is inscribed on the recording sheet (sample output is depicted in Figure 12) by a stylus mounted on the arm which is periodically lifted by an inner mechanism connected to the clockwork. A selector switch controls the frequency (0.5,

---

5   This experiment was a part of the very first doctoral dissertation in the history of experimental psychology.
6   http://history.psu.cas.cz/machinery/jaquet_graphic_chronometer.html
7   The simple variant without dials is called Jaquet's Chronograph.

1, 3, and 6 sec) in which the time marks are scratched. To ensure that the chronometer operates smoothly in both horizontal and vertical orientations, the instrument is equipped with a pressure spring which pushes the arm to its initial position. A horizontally positioned chronometer does not require any pressure spring, as the arm simply falls back to its initial position by means of gravity. Besides direct graphical recording, Jaquet's chronometer might also function as a switch in an electric circuit providing periodical electric impulses in a pre-set frequency.

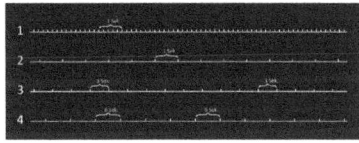

Figure 12. Sample recordings from Jaquet's Chronometer

Wundt's Chronograph

Chronograph nach Wundt (GE)

Figure 13. Wundt's Chronograph (Zimmermann, 1903)

Wundt's chronograph features simultaneous recording of multiple measurements together with a high precision time axis. In essence, the instrument is a combination of a chronograph with a rotating kymograph drum. The model[8] depicted in Figure 13 declares capability of capturing impressively small time intervals of 1/10 000 sec. The time axis is inscribed by a stylus (made of very light material such as beard hair) fixed to a vibrating tuning fork (see page 33). The vibration of the fork is maintained by an electromagnet placed between its arms.

---

8   Wundt (1909) notes that the Leipzig Institute had two chronographs constructed according to his own design proposal: an older type by Karl Krille and an improved version by E. Zimmermann.

As a recording medium the chronograph uses a sheet of paper wrapped around a revolving drum (with a length of 320 mm and a perimeter of 620 mm), covered with a layer of carbon black. The information from any sensory devices connected to the apparatus is traced by a set of markers with styluses. The drum movement is provided by clockwork propelled by a replaceable weight (up to 60 kg). Its rotation speed is regulated by means of decelerating air blades and selecting a proper size of the weight. The maximum rotation speed is limited to 10 revs/sec, which equals the speed of 6.2 m/sec. However, Hahn (1964) only states 1 m/sec as the maximum speed of record inscription in the carbon black. In general, the more precise the measurement needed, the faster the drum rotation speed that must be reached in order to obtain a readable time axis.

The carrier with styluses moves along the drum on rails and thus produces a spiral recording on the paper. The carrier is put in motion by a threaded bar which passes through the carrier and is rotated by the instrument's clockwork. To facilitate the movement, the carrier is also pulled by a steel cable with weight. It is probably worth mentioning that in order to achieve the highest precision possible the recording time cannot be very long; in fact, with the drum rotating at 10 revs/sec (to be able to read 10000 marks produced per second), the recording sheet is completely filled in less than one second.

Schumann's Chronograph

Chronograph nach Schumann (GE)

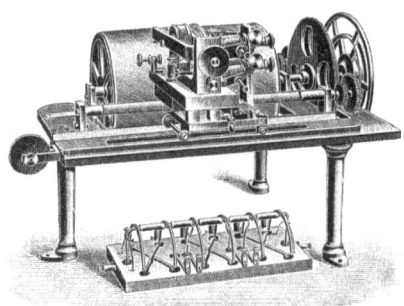

Figure 14. Schumann's Chronograph (Spindler & Hoyer, 1908)

The construction design is very similar to Wundt's chronograph. Schumann's variant is described in detail by Titchener (1895). The rotation of a horizontally positioned drum (230 mm in length and 500 mm in perimeter) is provided by an electromotor or a water motor. Besides these two the instrument can be propelled by a treadle sewing machine equipped with a flywheel.

Calibration Devices for Chronoscopes

The purpose of these devices is to provide exact time intervals as a criterion for calibration of instruments which are not capable of self-calibration (e.g. Hipp's Chronoscope). An exact time interval is calculated using the principle of a falling body of given mass. During the fall the object successively closes two contacts. Whereas the first electrical contact switches the tested chronoscope on, the second one causes the instrument to stop. The reliability of the tested chronoscope is evaluated on the degree of correspondence between the calculated time interval and the actual data supplied by the chronoscope. If a discrepancy is found, the chronoscope is adjusted and the procedure is repeated.

Naturally, to ensure maximal accurateness even these calibration devices need to be validated by comparison with chronographs operating on the principle of tuning forks. The chronograph inscribes a sinusoidal time axis in a black coal layer spread on a sheet of paper. The calibration device closes two contacts in the calculated moments and using an electromagnetic writer inscribes marks next to the time axis. Time determined by the sinusoid was then contrasted with the time interval set on the calibration device.

Large Falling Hammer Delay Timer

Grosser Kontrollhammer (GE)

Figure 15. Large Falling Hammer Delay Timer (Zimmermann, 1923d)

The main component of the device is a weight fixed to the end of an iron rod. The weight is held in the initial upper position by a solenoid attached to a tower-like stand. The duration of the fall is adjustable by varying the height of the solenoid and/or by shifting the counterweight. The axis around which the hammer rotates is set in a prism-shaped slot, and due to its minimal friction high precision is ensured. Straight direction without any lateral deflections of the hammer's fall is secured by sufficient length of the axis. There is an iron rod passing through the hammer head whose ends close the electrical contacts during the fall. The same function is also served by a slider attached to the hammer shaft. In the configuration in Figure 15 three contacts can be connected: two by means of the hammer head and a third one in the middle by means of the slider[9].

Contact Pendulum

Kontakt-Pendel (GE)

Figure 16.   Contact Pendulum (Zimmermann, 1903)

Contact pendulum is a simple device for closing several contacts in sequential but variable order. Before starting the measurement, the pendulum is held in its initial position by a solenoid. When released, the pendulum swings all the way to the other side, where it is caught and held still. During the swing the pendulum closes the contacts. All of the elements – the solenoid, the catcher, and the required number of contacts – can be arranged in any position on the swing path. The pendulum is equipped with two weights, one below the pendulum axis and the other one above it. The position of the weights on a millimeter scale along the pendulum arm determines the duration of the swing.

Impulse Generating Devices

These devices produce control impulses with adjustable frequencies, which were mainly used for generating time axes on graphical recordings. Another purpose, no less important than the previous one, was to control the change of stimuli in presentation devices.

---

9   The predecessor of the Large Falling Hammer was a simpler device called Pflüger Hammer. The models were similar in design, only the Pflüger Hammer lacked the slider on the hammer shaft. The Pflüger variant was often preferred to the more advanced Large Falling Hammer due to its lower purchase price.

Klemensiewicz's Air Pressure Transmission Chronograph

Transmissionschronograph nach Klemensiewicz (GE)

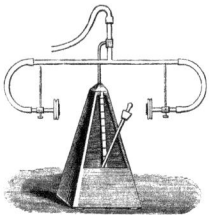

Figure 17. Klemensiewicz's Air Pressure Transmission Chronograph (Zimmermann, 1922b)

Klemensiewicz's apparatus is the only non-electric impulse generating device. A pendulum generates periodic pneumatic impulses by alternately hitting the right and the left air capsule (a variant of the Marey's tambour, see page 48). These impulses can be used for activation of other devices, or for producing time marks on the graphical recording. This design was a predecessor of a type of metronome with mercury contacts which served as sources of electric impulses.

Metronome with Electrical Interrupting Device

Metronom mit Quecksilberkontakten (GE)

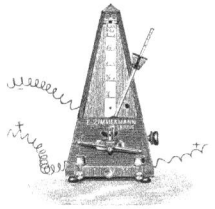

Figure 18. Metronome with Electrical Interrupting Device (Zimmermann, 1922b)

A metronome pendulum is connected with a horizontal lever beam. At the dead points, the corresponding contact at the end of the lever beam dips into a cup filled with mercury, closes the circuit and sends an electric impulse. In contrast to the standard solid metal contacts, the contacts in this elegant mercury-based solution do not wear, which means that the metronome does not slow down with use. The range of frequencies available depends on the type of metronome used. The metronome can also be supplemented with two solenoids that can stop the pendulum at any of the two dead points.

Simple Contact Clock

Einfache Kontaktuhr (GE)

Figure 19. Simple Contact Clock (Zimmermann, 1903)

This device is based on a traditional pendulum clock with a weight. The lever beam (placed horizontally above the clock face) is connected to the electric circuit. The clock pendulum tilts the beam whose ends alternately dip into two mercury cups, closing the circuit. An advantage over the metronome-based design is that the contact clock also provides information about the overall time elapsed.

Bowditch-Baltzar's Contact Clock

Kontaktuhr nach Bowditch-Baltzar (GE)

Figure 20. Bowditch-Baltzar's Contact Clocks (Zimmermann, 1912)

The improved version of a clock-based impulse generating device propelled by a weight is represented by Bowditch-Baltzar's contact clocks. In place of a clock face the device has a disc with 150 wooden pegs arranged in 10 concentric circles. The pegs moving in circles on the rotating disc periodically deflect the lever of a contact mechanism, alternately closing and opening the electric circuit. The selector switch at the bottom of the device enables the user to select the required frequency of impulses by shifting the contact mechanism to the circle with the corresponding number of pegs. The clock is thus able to generate ten different numbers (1, 2, 3, 4, 5, 10, 15, 20, 30, and 60) of alternations per minute.

Contact Pole Clock

This contact clock has neither a face nor hands. Instead, the axis of the minute hand carries a set of wheels with pegs. When the wheel is moving, these pegs sequentially close electrical contacts, generating impulses at regular intervals. The clock offers ten different frequencies (1, 2, 3, 4, 5, 10, 15, 20, 30, and 60 sec) by using ten wheels with different numbers of pegs. The target frequency is set by the positioning the slider with contacts against the corresponding wheel. The clockwork is propelled by a weight hidden inside the pole. The accuracy of the clockwork is adjusted by moving the adamantium weight along the ash pendulum bar (ash wood is used because of its low thermal and hygroscopic expansion coefficients).

Wundt's Timing Apparatus[10]

Taktierapparat nach Wundt (GE)

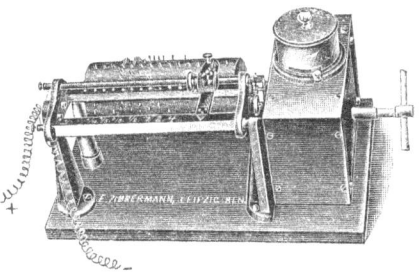

Figure 21. Wundt's Timing Apparatus (Zimmermann, 1922c)

The frequency of generated impulses is determined by the spacing of pegs on the perimeter of a metal drum. The drum has a rotation speed of 4 revs/sec. Constancy of the speed is secured by an inner centrifugal decelerating mechanism located in a vertical cylinder on top of a gear box. The pegs are arranged in 15 rows – 12 with

---

10   http://history.psu.cas.cz/machinery/wundt_timing_apparatus.html

regular spacing of pegs (for frequencies of 4, 2, 4/3, 1, 4/5, 2/3, 1/2, 2/5, 4/13, 1/5, 4/25, and 1/10 sec), and 3 with irregular spacing. The position of the slider against a particular row of pegs determines the frequency of impulses.

The actual impulse can be triggered by closing or breaking the electrical circuit. In one case, the slider acts as an independent contactor which is disconnected by each passing peg. In another case, the metal drum becomes a part of the electric circuit. The circuit is closed every time a peg touches the metal contact on the slider.

Bernstein's Spring (Cyclic) Interrupter

Federunterbrecher nach Bernstein (GE)

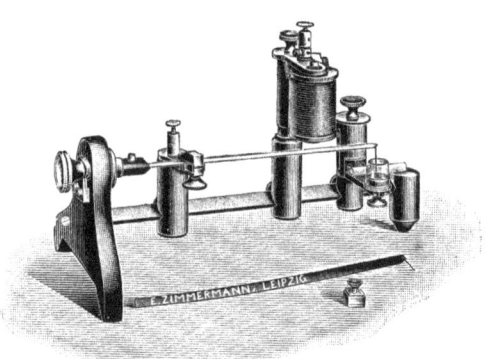

Figure 22. Bernstein's Spring (Cyclic) Interrupter (Zimmermann, 1904)

Bernstein's interrupter generates periodical breaks in an electric circuit with an adjustable frequency. The source of the frequency is a steel spring that is periodically attracted by an electromagnet. One end of the spring is fixed to the stand while the other is equipped with a platinum spike dipped in a cup filled with mercury. When the electric circuit is closed, the electromagnet lifts the spring up, the spike loses touch with the mercury, and the electric circuit is broken. When the electromagnet loses power, the spring returns back into its initial position, and according to Wagner's hammer principle, the process repeats itself periodically until power is provided. The instrument generates frequencies of 5, 10, 20, 25, 50, 100, and 250 Hz. The target frequency is set by replacing the spring with a stronger or weaker one, and/or changing the length of the oscillating part of the spring by moving the fixation anchor. When using the interrupter as a source of frequency for generating time axes, it is necessary to additionally connect the instrument to an electromagnetic registration device.

Meumann's Universal Contact Apparatus[11]

Universalkontakt-Apparat nach Meumann (GE)

Figure 23. Meumann's Universal Contact Apparatus (Zimmermann, 1903)

 This device enables setting a unique sequence of time intervals between impulses. The main component of the instrument is a metal wheel with a perimeter of 280 mm and an arc degree scale inscribed on its diameter. The contacts placed around the wheel's perimeter are successively closed by a contact finger at the end of a revolving arm. The exact location of each contact is calculated from the required time interval between the impulses and the angular velocity of the arm.

The bearing pivot located in the center of the wheel carries a revolving contact arm connected with a stepped transmission through a set of cogwheels. The whole system is driven by an external source (e.g. a kymograph, see page 37) by means of a leather belt attached around one of the three transmission gears.

The instrument was typically delivered with three types of contacts. The sliding triangle contact is used for generating single impulses. The duration of the impulses can be adjusted by rearranging the contact finger on the arm (using a micrometer screw) so that it moves either across the wider or the thinner part of the triangle's surface. The rotating switch for permanent circuit closure, on the other hand, allows alternate switching between two electric circuits, which are switched once with each revolution of the arm. Finally, the absolute momentary contact is able to produce short-term breaks in a permanent current flowing through the electric circuit.

---

11 http://history.psu.cas.cz/machinery/meumann_universal_contact_apparatus.html

Reaction Keys

Apart from time measuring instruments and stimulus presentation devices, experiments with reaction time also require tools which secure transmission of the test subject's response to the recording device. In this chapter we present an overview of the most typical designs of these tools. In general, reaction keys can be divided into three basic types depending on the way they are activated: hand-operated, acoustic, and lip keys. Hand-operated keys, when activated, control the closing or breaking of an electric circuit to which other instruments (like chronographs or exposition devices) are connected. Acoustic and lip keys are designed for experiments that require detection of the exact moment of a verbal response. They proved to be useful, for example, in association experiments involving response latency measurement (e.g. Titchener, 1905; Cattell, 1886b). Most reaction keys have electrical contacts protected with small platinum[12] plates to prevent wear and extend the key's lifespan.

Simple Reaction Key

Einfacher Reaktionstaster (GE)

Figure 24. Simple Reaction Key (Zimmermann, 1928)

This type of the reaction key is only used for closing a circuit. The depressed key is pushed up to its original position by a small metal plate, which means that pressing the key might require considerable effort.

---

12 Platinum is an inert metal with a particularly high melting point (1768°C).

Simple Reaction Key by Zimmermann

Einfacher Reaktionstaster nach Zimmermann (GE)

Figure 25. Simple Reaction Key by Zimmermann (Zimmermann, 1923e)

Zimmermann's reaction key closes or breaks the electric circuit when its button is pressed. Moreover, additional devices can be connected to the key by means of a permanent switch, which enables fast and easy activation or deactivation of the device. Sensitivity of the key can be adjusted by a pressure bolt located above the arm of the button.

Telegraph Key (American Model)

Reaktionstaster (Telegraphentaster) (GE)

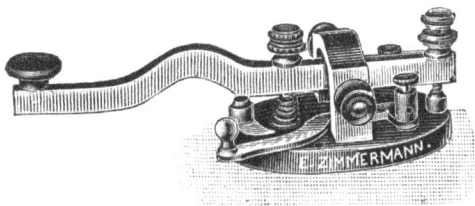

Figure 26. Telegraph Key (American Model) (Zimmermann, 1923e)

The telegraph key was designed to minimize the motor activity needed to hold the key down. It works on the principle of a simple lever with a prolonged arm. The key is characterized by high sensitivity to finger movement, which can be further adjusted by a pressure bolt. During the maintenance and inspection of the experimental set, the key can be permanently bypassed by a brass strip. Due to the typical shape of the arm the key was also referred to as a 'camelback'.

Reaction Switch with Platinum Contact and Air Capsule

Reaktionstaster mit Luftkapsel (GE)

Figure 27. Reaction Switch with Platinum Contact and Air Capsule (Zimmermann, 1923e)

This notable device enables interconnection of pneumatic and electric instruments in a single set. Holding down the button simultaneously closes an electric circuit and exerts pressure to a rubber air capsule. This way it is possible to generate both electric and pneumatic impulses at the same time. The key is also a good indicator of pressure decreases in the pneumatic system. When pressure is decreased, the air capsule shrinks down, and the arm sitting on the capsule descends and closes the contacts, producing an electric impulse. The device was mainly used in conjunction with an olfactometer (see page 90) or a pneumograph (see page 97).

Ten-fold Finger Reaction Apparatus with Stopper Contacts

Zehnfacher Reaktionsapparat mit Stöpsel-Kontakten (GE)

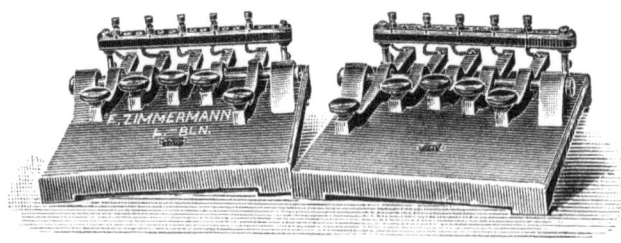

Figure 28. Ten-fold Finger Reaction Apparatus with Stopper Contacts (Zimmermann, 1896)

This set of ten ergonomically arranged keys allows the user to close an electric circuit by any of the ten fingers. The instrument was used mainly in learning experiments. Titchener (1895) refers to a specific variant of this apparatus in which the keys are supplemented with non-insulated contacts that can apply mild stimulus electric shocks, generated by a secondary induction coil, to any of the test subject's fingertips.

Römer's Acoustic Switch: Apparatus for Acoustic Stimulation and Response

Schallschlüssel nach Römer, akustischer Reiz- und Reaktionsapparat (GE)

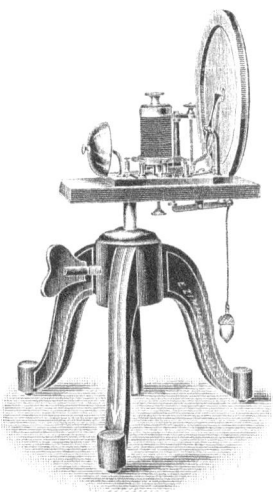

Figure 29. Römer's Acoustic Switch: Apparatus for Acoustic Stimulation and Response (Zimmermann, 1928)

The main component of this reaction key is a membrane made of a very thin plate of isinglass, metal, or wood veneer. In the center of the reverse surface of the membrane there is a small target attached with a platinum contact. Another spiked platinum contact is positioned against the target. The test subject must speak very close to the membrane, so that the loudly spoken verbal answer can vibrate the membrane and disconnect the spiked contact from the target. When the circuit is broken (as announced by the ring of a bell), the instrument's electromagnet is switched off, releasing an anchor. This anchor subsequently closes a circuit connecting the associated devices. Before launching another trial it is necessary to set the device into its initial position by means of a pull string.

It is probably worth mentioning that as an experimental tool, Römer's acoustic switch met with a rather critical response on the part of the scientific public (Woodworth, Schlosberg, 1959), as it was not able to detect answers that were not loud enough.

Cattell's Acoustic Switch

Schallschlüssel nach Cattell (GE)

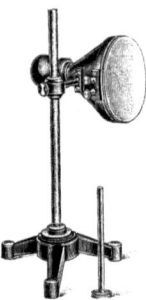

Figure 30. Cattell's Acoustic Switch (Spindler & Hoyer, 1908)

Cattell's key also uses a membrane for the transformation of a spoken response into an electric impulse. In this case, however, the membrane's sensitivity is ensured by high elasticity material (lamb skin or latex). When the verbal response is spoken into the mouthpiece, the contact on the curved membrane is pulled apart from the spiked contact fixed to a tube, and the electric circuit is broken.

The vibrating membrane naturally produces a series of electric impulses. To filter out the redundant subsequent impulses, the device can be supplied with an electromagnetic relay which keeps the circuit permanently open after the first impulse is produced.

Lip Key

Lippenschlüssel (GE)

Figure 31. Lip Key (Zimmermann, 1923e)

The purpose of the lip key is the same as that of acoustic switches, but this tool is based on different principle. While acoustic switches transform work with acoustic waves, the lip key detects mechanical movement of the mouth. In the initial setting the test subject keeps the brass arms pressed together between their lips.

To make the experience more comfortable for the test subject, as well as to increase the durability of the device, the mouthpiece was typically crafted from ivory. When the person opens their mouth to pronounce the verbal response, the arms of the key are pushed apart by a spring positioned between them. The movement of the arms results in breaking or closing of the circuit (depending on the type of electric connection).

Meumann's dental key variant detects movements of the jaws. It is equipped with an additional arresting mechanism, which prevents repetitive pressing of the key. The arresting mechanism has to be dislodged before the subsequent trial.

Tuning Forks

Even though tuning forks are primarily considered as acoustic devices, early experimental psychologists used them mainly as sources of high-frequency oscillations for various time recording and time measuring devices.

The original tuning fork (a steel U-shaped bar) was invented by the British musician John Shore. When struck, the fork vibrates in a constant frequency, emitting a specific pure sound (after the initial high overtones die down).

In the second half of the 19th century the main European manufacturer of tuning forks was the Koenig Company in Paris. When looking at the inventory lists of the early psychological laboratories (Münsterberg, 1893; Draaisma, 1992), virtually in any of them at least one item supplied by Rudolph Koenig can be spotted. Koenig's prominent position in the tuning fork market is also confirmed by Pisko (1865) in his book devoted to acoustic instruments in scientific experiments. Rudolph Koenig closely cooperated with H. Helmholtz, as documented by the correspondence preserved by the Berlin-Brandenburg Academy of Sciences.

Simple Tuning Fork

Stimmgabel (GE)

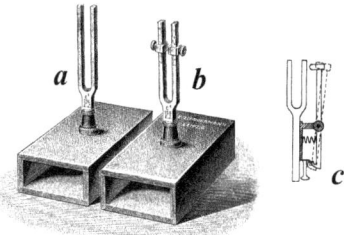

Figure 32. Variants of simple tuning fork (Zimmermann, 1903; Spindler & Hoyer, 1908)

Simple tuning forks are mainly intended for acoustic and demonstration purposes. Therefore, they are often supplemented with wooden resonant boxes. They were produced by many manufacturers in several variants (Lanc, 1966): the very basic tuning forks (letter *a* in Figure 32); tuning forks with millimeter or musical scales and sliding weights for setting the frequency of the fork in a predefined range (letter *b* in Figure 32); and tuning forks with hammers securing constant strength of the strikes (letter *c* in Figure 32).

Electromagnetic Tuning Fork

Elektromagnetische Stimmgabel (GE)

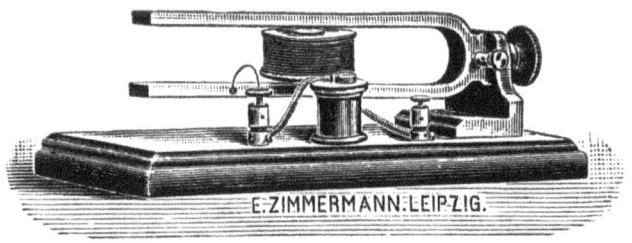

Figure 33. Electromagnetic Tuning Fork (Zimmermann, 1928)

Electromagnetic tuning fork has the ability to maintain constant amplitude of vibration using the principle of Wagner's hammer. The device consists of a U-shaped tuning fork and a solenoid positioned between[13] its prongs. When the solenoid receives electric current, the prongs are drawn towards it. The contact located on the lower prong is detached from the platinum contact on the base and breaks the current flow. Consequently, the solenoid stops attracting the prongs, which are swung in the opposite direction. As they swing back, the circuit is closed again, and the process continues repetitively until the electric power source is turned off. While the frequency of the fork remains constant, the amplitude can be altered by changing the amperage. Hence, the device can be supplemented with a rheostat for continuous amperage adjustment.

---

13   In a technologically more convenient design of the tuning fork the prongs were positioned between the arms of a U-shaped electromagnet (e.g. Helmholtz's variant from 1870).

Electromagnetic Tuning Fork with Mercury Contact

Elektromagnetische Stimmgabel belieb. Schwingungszahl (GE)

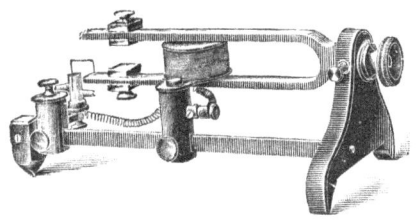

Figure 34. Electromagnetic Tuning Fork with Mercury Contact (Zimmermann, 1896)

Electromagnetic tuning fork with a standard solid contact is highly vulnerable to material fatigue, which might result in potential malfunctioning. The depicted design of electromagnetic tuning fork uses a vertically adjustable mercury cup and a platinum wire as contacts. Both prongs are equipped with slide weights whose position determines the frequency of vibration.

In addition to that, this model can make use of a wider range of amperage, since the slide solenoid can change its position to avoid unwanted collisions with the prongs.

Electromagnetic Tuning Fork with Resonance Tube

Elektromagnetische Stimmgabel mit Rezonator (GE)

Figure 35. Electromagnetic Tuning Fork with Resonance Tube (Helmholtz, 1870)

This tuning fork is primarily used as an acoustic device. All its components (tuning fork, electromagnet and resonance tube) are mounted on a solid wooden base, which is underlaid with hose pipes to ensure sufficient isolation. To obtain clear, strong and pure sound, the resonance tube needs to be properly positioned against the tuning fork. The sound can be instantly muted by covering the input opening of the tube.

Gutzmann's Tuning Fork Apparatus

Stimmgabel–Apparat nach Gutzmann (GE)

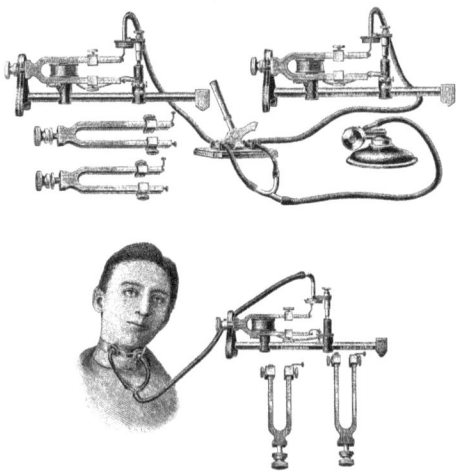

Figure 36. Gutzmann's Tuning Fork Apparatus (Zimmermann, 1912). Down – the set for correction of vocal cords functionality; up – the set for tactile differentiating experiments.

Gutzmann's apparatus was delivered in two different sets according to the particular purpose (Zimmermann, 1928). The first set comprises four electromagnetic tuning forks with slide weights (for setting target notes and half notes in the range from A to a1), a holder with a moveable solenoid, platinum contacts and Marey's tambour, and Zünd-Burquet's laryngograph. Vibrations from the tuning fork are transmitted through Marey's tambour to the laryngograph attached to the subject's neck. This method of the vocal cord stimulation was used to rectify functional voice disorders.

The other set was designed as a tool for the research of minimum discernible differences in stimulus intensity. It contains eight tuning forks with slide weights, two holders, a pneumatic switch and a terminal tambour. Vibrations from the selected tuning fork are transmitted to the terminal tambour which serves as tactile interface for the test subject. Different sources of vibration are selected using a switch which leaves the pneumatic main from the preferred tuning fork open while blocking the other ones.

Electromagnetic Tuning Fork (for direct time measurement)

Elektromagnetische Stimmgabel (direkten Zeitschreibung) (GE)

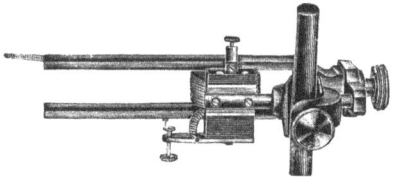

Figure 37. Electromagnetic Tuning Fork (for direct time measurement) (Zimmermann, 1904)

For the purpose of graphical depiction of time lines, this tuning fork variant is equipped with a stylus fixed to the tip of one of the prongs. The stylus inscribes the vibrations into a carbon black layer spread on a paper belt wrapped around a kymograph (see page 37).

Recording Devices

Kymographs

The invention of kymograph is associated with the name of German physiologist Carl Ludwig, who created it in 1847 as an instrument for monitoring and recording changes in arterial blood pressure. Originally, a device of such type was called kymatographion. One reference to such an instrument can be found in a footnote by Arnold (1858) in his Report on the Physiology Department of the University of Heidelberg. In the report, which includes a complete listing of apparatus used at the Physiology Department, Arnold points out the changes he made in the construction of the kymatographion, which were incorporated by the mechanic Keinath of Tübingen into the original design by Ludwig and Volkmann. The device was later referred to as 'kymographion' (Cyon, 1876a). Otto Lanc (1966) still uses the term kymographion, but he already mentions the possibility of abbreviating the name to 'kymograph', which is also the term we are using throughout this book, since it is nowadays the most commonly used expression. Yet, from the historical perspective, it might be more accurate to stick to the original title.

We will describe the functioning of the kymograph on Ludwig-Baltzar's kymograph variant, which we consider as the basic and original variant of the device, a prototype of all other variants.

Ludwig–Baltzar's Kymograph

Ludwig–Baltzar'sches Kymographion (GE)

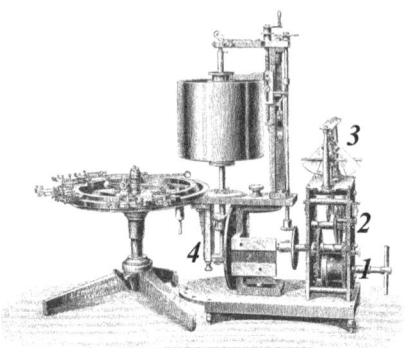

Figure 38. Ludwig–Baltzar's Kymograph (Zimmermann, 1903)

Kymograph is a device designed to record the course of experiments in a graphical form. At present, even though we hardly ever come across a kymograph when conducting psychological research, it is still used in other scientific fields such as geology, e.g. in the construction of seismographs. The kymograph can concurrently also serve as a propellant unit, as depicted in Zimmermann's catalogue (1903), driving the previously described Meumann's universal contact apparatus. In other words, the kymograph in this case does not only fulfill its primary role of a record–taking mechanism, but its cogged wheels also serve as the arm of Meumann's switch spin.

The main part of the kymograph is a replaceable drum onto which the record sheet is placed. The drum is propelled by clockwork, and the number of revolutions can be set within the range of one rev in 2 seconds up to one rev in 1.5 hours. The revolution speed can be adjusted through the variation of four different parameters: First, choosing between two springs of different stiffness (*1* in fig. 38); second, combining the inner gearings of the clockwork machine (*2* in fig. 38); third, adjusting the settings of Foucault's regulator (*3* in fig. 38); and fourth, setting a friction gear mechanism right on the axis of the drum (*4* in fig. 38).

Foucault's regulator is the most complicated part of the apparatus in terms of construction. When the clockwork mechanism is wound up to its maximum, the rotation of the kymograph's drum is fast, but then it gradually slows down until the clockwork winds down and stops. The purpose of Foucault's regulator is to keep the rotation of the drum constant. When the rotation speed is high, the centrifugal force pulls out the free blades of the regulator and slows down the rotation through the effect of air resistance. Simpler kymographs were equipped, instead of the rather expensive Foucault's regulator, with a cheaper replaceable blade (i.e. a shaped metal plate). Less sophisticated variants of the kymograph typically make use of only one single parameter for the adjustment of speed, which is usually represented by the friction gear mechanism. In this case, the driving force of the clockwork is transferred to the kymograph by means of two discs, which are assembled perpendicularly to each other. The closer the propelling disc is set to the center of the kymograph's disc, the faster the rotation speed of the drum.

Another important feature of Ludwig-Baltzar's kymograph is the possibility of vertical movement of the drum. The movement can be either controlled manually by whirling a handle on the top of the kymograph, or it can be automatically transmitted from the clockwork by means of an auxiliary feed shaft. This mechanism enables the movement of the drum towards the base, so that the recording is inscribed in the form of a helix. This method of inscription has helped to significantly increase the maximum recording time during measurements.

In the following paragraphs we will introduce other main variants of the kymograph, namely school kymograph, universal kymograph of Zimmermann's design, Wundt's kymograph, kymograph with endless paper, and large weight-driven kymograph, plus their basic accessories.

School Kymograph (with Clockwork and Friction Gearing)[14]

Federkymographion ohne Uhrwerk und Friktionsverstellung mit Schleuder (GE)

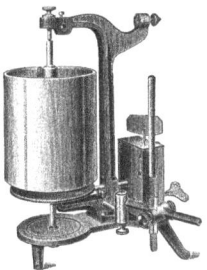

Figure 39: School Kymograph (Zimmermann, 1923a)

 Principally, this is the simplest variant of kymograph. A robust cast iron construction allows using the kymograph in both vertical and horizontal position. A spring hidden in the hollow of the upper fixation knob forces the kymograph's disc against the propelling disc, transferring rotation from the clockwork to the drum.

---

14   http://history.psu.cas.cz/machinery/school_kymograph.html

The instrument is called 'School kymograph' because of its low price and almost indestructible heavy construction.

Kymograph with Endless Paper

Kymographion für fortlaufendes Papier (GE)

Figure 40. Kymograph with Endless Paper (Zimmermann, 1903)

This kymograph is intended for long-term recording of the quantities measured. Moreover, when faster movement of the writing medium is needed (i.e. there are many actions to be recorded in a short time period), this kymograph proves to be a particularly useful device. On the sides of the device there are two pins attached. At the beginning of the measurement, one pin holds a roll of paper, while the paper head is passed through a set of tensioning rollers to the second pin. The schema depicts the location of the two pins, as well as the tensioning mechanism, which provides a 65 mm section of flat paper. At this flat section the nibs of the writing tool are applied. The writing tool uses ink instead of scraping into a layer of soot. The more common method of scraping cannot be used here, since the obtained recording would likely be damaged as the paper is reeled in.

Universal Kymograph

Universal Kymographion (GE)

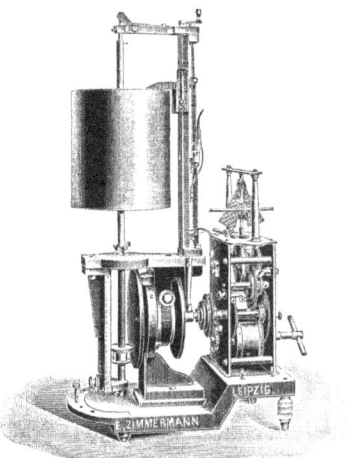

Figure 41. Universal Kymograph (Zimmermann, 1900)

The universal kymograph was delivered with a drum 180 mm in height. The device enables automatic movement of the drum up to two thirds of its height, which can vary between 2 and 50 millimeters per revolution. The rotation speed can be adjusted in the range from 2 seconds to 90 minutes per revolution. A full stretch of the propelling flat spring provides approximately 1.5 hours of running time.

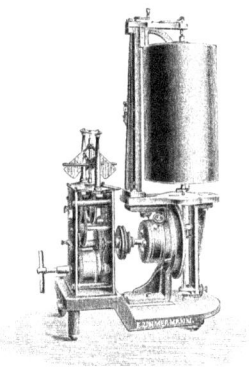

Figure 42. An Extra Tall Drum Installed on the Universal Kymograph (Zimmermann, 1900)

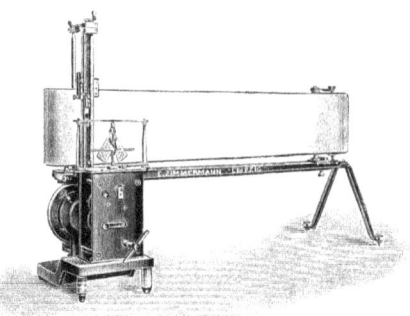

Figure 43.   Universal Kymograph with Prolonged Arm (Zimmermann, 1900)

Figure 44.   Universal Kymograph with Endless Paper (Zimmermann, 1900)

The universality of this design allows installing various accessories on the device to satisfy researchers' special needs. In case of long-lasting experiments it is possible to attach an external propelling device to prolong the running time of the kymograph. Experiments with many simultaneous data sources require a wide recording surface for a considerably large set of styluses lined up parallel to each other. To meet the needs of such experiments, it is possible to replace the original drum with an extra tall one (300 mm in height). Naturally, the use of a taller drum makes further vertical movement impossible. In some cases, for example, in experiments producing data with high frequency of incidents, the standard 50 cm paper length (limited by the drum's perimeter) can be insufficient. For this reason, Zimmermann came up with a prolonged arm which allowed using a paper belt with the length of 2.5 m. Another accessory resolving the same issue is the 'endless' paper mechanism. A roll of endless paper is slid onto a pin with a slight curb (to avoid paper droop). The paper belt runs from the roll to the kymograph's drum, where the recording is performed. The paper is then reeled up on another pin. To avoid tearing of the paper, the machine is equipped with a speed compensator, which adjusts the rotation speed of the reeling pin according to the actual amount of wound paper. The device can be used in both vertical and horizontal positions. In addition, the direction of the paper movement can be reversed if necessary (from left to right and vice versa).

Wundt's Kymograph

Kymographion nach Wundt (GE)

Figure 45. Wundt's Kymograph (Zimmermann, 1903)

Wund't kymograph was originally designed for the measurement of volume changes in various parts of the human body. Its maximum speed is limited to 100 mm per second (with a 500 mm perimeter, the drum makes one revolution in five seconds). The rotation speed can be continuously adjusted using friction gearing. Vertical movement of a slider (inserted in a prismatic track) with a set of styluses is secured by a rotating threaded bar, whose rotation is derived from the main axis of a clockwork mechanism. The initial position of the slider can be set manually by means of a handle located on the top of the threaded bar. The outcome recording is in the shape of a helix. When the paper is removed and spread out, several sets of ascending curves are visible.

Large Weight-Driven Kymograph

Grosses Gewichts-Kymographion (GE)

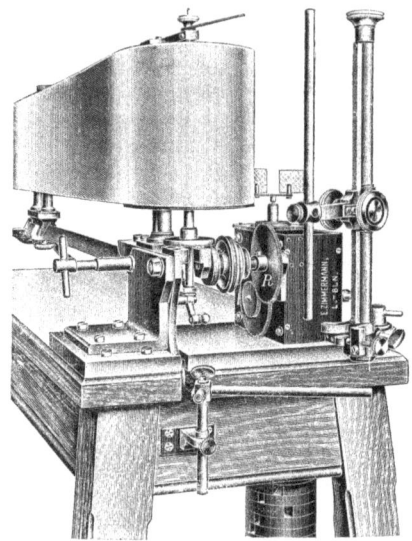

Figure 46. Large Weight-Driven Kymograph (Zimmermann, 1928)

This kymograph uses a long paper loop as the recording medium. It is driven by a hanging weight. The speed of the paper movement can be set within the range between 0.5 and 100 mm per second by using different weights. The tensioning drum can be positioned up to 2.5 m away from the recording drum. The device also offers the possibility to erect the arm to a vertical position. This makes the preparation and finalizing procedures with the paper medium easier (i.e. application of the carbon black layer before the experiment and fixation of the recording with shellac[15] afterwards).

Kymograph Accessories

Various accessories supplied by instrument manufacturers served as helpful tools in setting up the experiment and subsequent preservation of data recordings. These tools were mostly inteded to make the maintanance work more efficient and less demanding.

---

15 Shellac is a type of resin made from the secretion of the female lac bug.

Recording Drum on Stand

Registriertrommel auf Stativ (GE)

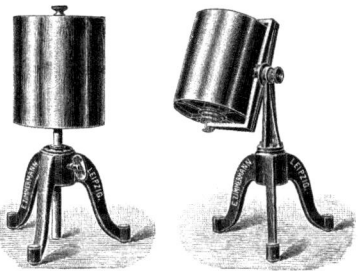

Figure 47. Recording Drums on Stand (Zimmermann, 1896). Simple variant of stand on the left; vertically and horizontally adjustable version on the right.

To make experimental work more efficient, manufacturers offered spare drums. These standard-size drums could be delivered with various stands. While the simplest stand only allowed fixation on a vertical spindle, the more elaborated models offered both vertical and horizontal positioning of the drum for a more comfortable manipulation with the recording media.

Lamp-Blacking Frame According to von Frey

Berussgestell nach von Frey (GE)

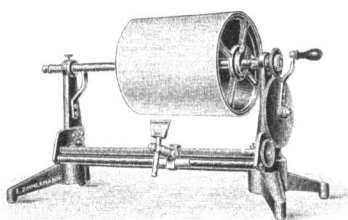

Figure 48. Lamp-Blacking Frame According to von Frey (Zimmermann, 1912)

This stand, designed by physiologist Maximilian von Frey, is primarily used for covering paper sheets with a layer of carbon black. The drum wrapped in the sheet of paper is fixed on shaft, which is driven manually using a wheel handle. An appropriate rotation speed is ensured by mechanical gearing. The researcher or his/her assistant smoothly moves a candle, or other source of soot, beneath the rotating drum. More recent variants of the stand are supplied with a gas burner which is automatically moved along the bottom of the drum. To ensure sufficient production of soot, the gas passes through a piece of gauze impregnated with benzene. It is important to always make sure that the paper sheet is fixed tightly around the drum, whose metal body conducts away the heat; otherwise, the paper sheet can flare up (personal experience, 2002). To make the process of paper blacking even more efficient, there are also stands with wide-format burners extended along the whole drum.

Lamp-Blacking Frame for Hering Loops

Berussgestell für Hering'sche Schleifen (GE)

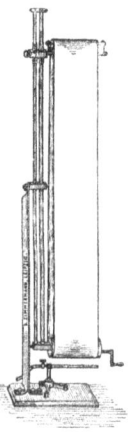

Figure 49. Lamp-Blacking Frame for Hering Loops (Zimmermann, 1921b)

Kymographs using a Hering loop on a prolonged arm or those using endless paper require a special design of the lamp-blacking stand. It has a characteristic tall construction which is needed for stretching out the whole length of the paper belt. After the blackening procedure is finished, the paper belt must be removed from the stand and carefully set up directly on the kymograph.

Fixation Apparatus

Fixiereinrichtung (GE)

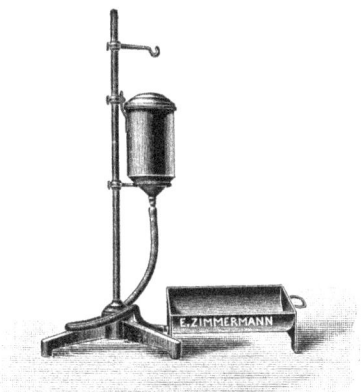

Figure 50. Fixation Apparatus (Zimmermann, 1903)

It is evident that the carbon black layer is extremely vulnerable to mechanical damage. Therefore, experimental recording inscribed in it must be protected and preserved for later analyses by a specific fixation procedure in which the recording is covered with a protective film. The drum with the recording is dunked into a correspondingly shaped tub filled with a fixation liquid (typically a shellac/ alcohol solution). The drum is then slowly rotated in the tub so that the whole paper sheet is soaked. The fixation liquid is stored in a tank. Before the fixation procedure begins, the liquid is siphoned from a higher positioned tank on a stand to the tub through a rubber hose. After the procedure is finished, the tank is moved below the tub allowing the remaining liquid to flow back into the tank and be saved for further use.

Registration Devices

All experimental work depends on the possibility of adequate representation of the measured variables. A typical experimental recording set in the early laboratories consisted of three main components: an input sensory device (e.g. reaction key), a registration device, and a kymograph. Registration devices transform impulses detected by different kinds of sensors into analyzable graphical records. Based on the way in which the impulses are transmitted, recording devices can be divided into three basic groups: pneumatic, mechanic, and electro-mechanic.

Pneumatic Registration Devices

Pneumatic registration devices respond to the change of air pressure inside the system.

Marey's Tambour

Marey'sche Tamboure (GE)

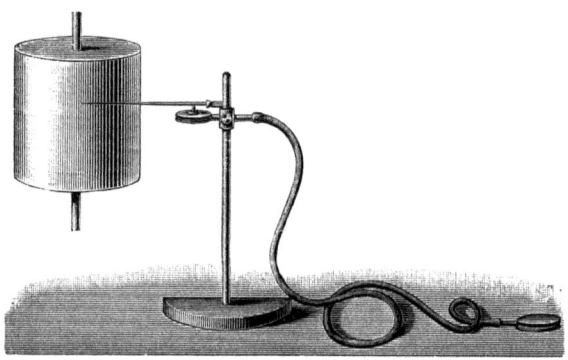

Figure 51. Marey's Tambour (Langendorff, 1891)

Most of pneumatic registration devices are based on the principle of Marey's tambour. A simple version of Marey's tambour consists of a metal circular shell with an elastic membrane stretched on the top, fastened by an ecru thread tied up in the depression on the side of the shell. The metal body of the tambour is connected to a pneumatic line. When the air pressure inside the experimental pneumatic system is increased, the tambour's membrane puffs out. The vertical movement of the membrane is then mechanically transmitted to a marker which oscillates over a recording medium. A thin metal plate is attached to the membrane to protect it as well as to facilitate the pneumatic-mechanic transmission. Sealing wax was often used as a binder between the metal plate and the membrane because of its good adhesion properties and because it did not etch the rubber material of the membrane.

The simplest experimental recording set with a registration device based on Marey's tambours is depicted in Figure 51. Pressing on the input tambour causes an increase in air pressure and consequent bulging of the membrane of the output tambour. The marker connected to the tambour is lifted up, drawing the recording curve. The more the input tambour is pressed, the higher the air pressure in the system, and the bigger the amplitude of the curve.

Figure 52. Marey's Tambour with Adjustable Amplitude of Recording Curve (Zimmermann, 1903)

A more advanced model of Marey's tambour (see Figure 52) is capable of controlling the size of the amplitude of the recording curve. The amplitude size is set by a micrometric screw which adjusts the position of the tambour along the arm of the marker. Moving the tambour closer to the marker's point produces lower amplitude, while moving it in the opposite direction (closer to the joint of the arm) increases it. Another micrometric screw adjusts the pressure of the marker against the recording medium to obtain a clear trail. Cyon (1876a) also mentions a less elaborated version of the tambour with adjustable amplitude without the micrometric control of the exact position of the tambour.

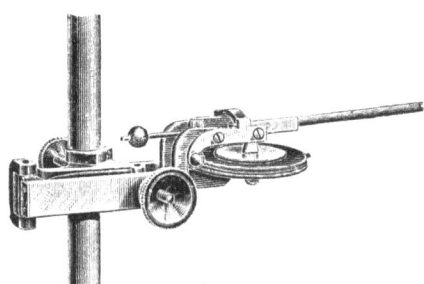

Figure 53. Marey's Tambour with Adjustable Amplitude and Balanced Lever Beam (Zimmermann, 1903)

Zimmermann (1903) offers an even more sophisticated version of Marey's tambour incorporating micrometric control of both the tambour's position and the marker's pressure force. Moreover, it has a sliding balance weight located behind the joint of the lever beam which reduces the force needed to raise the marker and thus makes the registration device more sensitive. To eliminate the risk of membrane penetration during installation by a sudden change in air pressure, the device is equipped with a safety shutoff.

Piston Registering Apparatus

Pistonrekorder (GE)

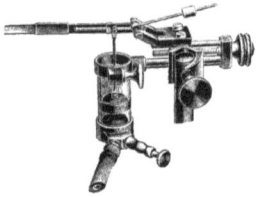

Figure 54. Piston Registering Apparatus (Zimmermann, 1903)

Piston registering apparatus is useful when a considerable amount of air must be handled by the experimental recording set. The main component of the device is a tube made of polished glass with a hard rubber piston inside. The incoming air lifts up the piston, which is connected through a double-joint connecting rod with a balanced lever beam carrying a marker. The device is provided with a micrometric screw for adjusting the position of the piston tube against the lever beam to set the amplitude size of the recorded curve. In addition, the device is equipped with a regulation point to set the initial position of the piston inside the glass tube.

Wavograph According to Fick

Wellenzeichner nach Fick (GE)

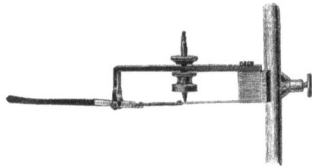

Figure 55. Wavograph According to Fick (Zimmermann, 1903)

Fick's device is primarily intended for the registration of heart activity. Pressure impulses from the sensor are conducted through a rubber hose to Marey's tambour, which has a spike attached to its membrane. In the zero position, the spike touches an elastic spring connected to the marker lever. With the increase in the air pressure, the spike pushes against the spring, deflecting the marker. As the pressure decreases, the elastic spring returns the marker into its initial position. The marker is made of straw. The length of the straw determines the amplitude of the recorded curve.

EXPERIMENTAL EQUIPMENT 51

Mechanic Registration Devices

Mechanic registration devices transmit impulses from sensory instruments to the marker by mechanic connections, such as connecting rods, cords, chains, etc.

Universal Marking Lever

Universal-Schreibhebel (GE)

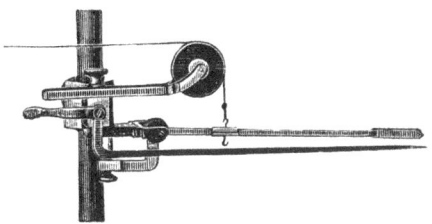

Figure 56. Universal Marking Lever (Zimmermann, 1903)

Impulses from the sensory device are conveyed by a cord hung over a pulley. The cord is connected to a slider on 15 cm arm carrying a marker. The adjustable position of the slider (and the pulley) influences the amplitude size of the recorded curve. To facilitate the return of the arm to its initial position, a counterweight can be set against the traction force of the cord. When the device is used in a vertical position, the counterweight can be substituted for a spring.

Vertical Marking Apparatus

Vertikalschreiber (GE)

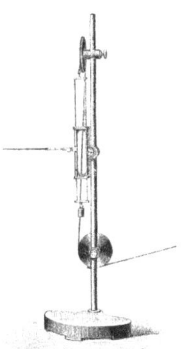

Figure 57. Vertical Marking Apparatus (Zimmermann, 1912)

Vertical marking apparatus is mainly used for the registration of ergographic measurements by a vertical kymograph. Horizontal movement of the cord coming from the sensory device is transformed into vertical movement by a pair of pulleys. The marker is fixed to a slider which is pulled up with every incoming impulse. To the bottom of the slider there is a weight attached which pulls the slider down into its initial position and also maintains appropriate tension in the cord.

Electromechanic Recording Devices

Recording devices based on electromechanic connections are especially helpful when the distance between the sensor and the marker is so long that both pneumatic and mechanic transmission of impulses would suffer considerable degradation.

Double Magnet Marker

Doppel-Markiermagnet (GE)

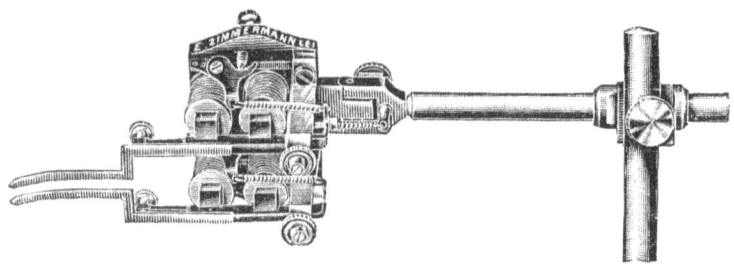

Figure 58. Double Magnet Marker (Zimmermann, 1903)

This recording device is designed for the recording of two independent signals at the same time. Basically, it consists of two identical electromagnetic devices combined into a single unit with a common micrometric screw for the adjustment of the markers' pressure against the drum. Electrical impulses from the sensory device turn on the corresponding electromagnet, which deflects one of the markers. The deflected marker is then drawn back into its initial position by a spring. There are also units with three or four markers working on the same principle. The major advantage of these multiple-marker devices over a set of single-unit markers is a more compact construction and easier adjustment of the markers' positions.

Signal Marker Pen according to Pfeil

Federsignal nach Pfeil (GE)

Figure 59. Signal Marker Pen according to Pfeil (Zimmermann, 1912)

The primary function of Pheil's device is the recording of a time axis generated by an electromagnetic tuning fork with the frequency up to 250 Hz. The device can provide magnification of the oscillation amplitude up to twenty times of the original amplitude size. Thanks to its robust construction and a substantially large electromagnet, the apparatus also functions with a relatively strong current, which decreases latency and minimizes degradations in the input signal. The high capacity of the device also enables setting higher pressure of the marker against the kymograph's drum and thus produces recordings of high readability.

Vibrating Pen

Schwingende Feder (GE)

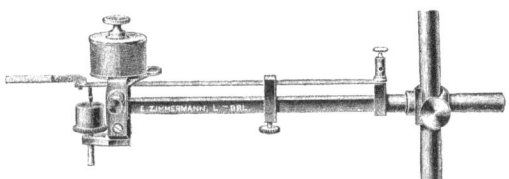

Figure 60. Vibrating Pen (Zimmermann, 1912)

The vibrating pen is used for creating and recording of a time axis. Oscillations are generated on the principle of Wagner's hammer. When the electromagnet is turned on, it lifts up a steel spring with a marker fixed to its end. This movement pulls out the contact from a mercury cup, breaking the electric circuit. With the electromagnet turned off, the spring returns back to its initial position and the contact in mercury cup is closed again. The frequency of oscillation is controlled by the position of a fixation anchor, which adjusts the length of the oscillating section of the spring.

Marey's Chronograph

Chronograph nach Marey (GE)

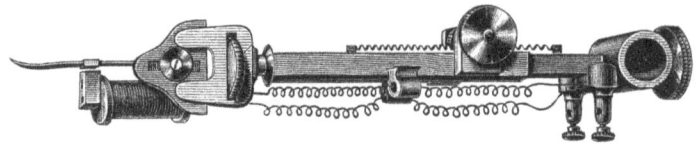

Figure 61. Marey's Chronograph (Langendorff, 1891)

Marey's chronograph obtains working frequency from external sources, such as an electromagnetic tuning fork or Bernstein's interrupter. The received impulses power the electromagnet, which deflects an anchor with the marker. The advantage of Marey's chronograph's design is that its marker can easily be aligned with the markers of other registration devices by means of a telescopic arm.

Accessories for Registration Devices

Writing Utensils for Registrations

Schreibutensilien (GE)

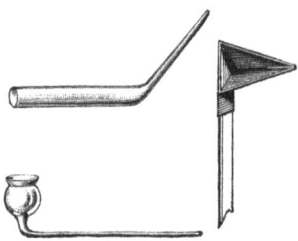

Figure 62. Writing Utensils for Registrations (Langendorff, 1891)

The recordings of data from sensory and time devices can be made in the form of an ink trace or an inscription into a carbon black layer. Glass pipettes can be used for drawing a thin ink curve on a paper medium. They consist of a small ink tank and a discharge pipe with a 0.1 to 0.15 mm outflow hole. Besides glass, the writing tool can be made of a nickelled brass sheet shaped into a triangular dish with a thin capillary aperture. Such tools are capable of producing a very thin ink line.

One of the most reliable (although a little bit old-school) way of recording data is the inscription into a layer of carbon black applied on varnished paper. The outcome recording is hence represented by a set of multiple parallel white curves on a black background. The markers have to be both lightweight and solid at the same time. Eligible materials include bamboo, straw, goose quill, or aluminum.

Electropneumatic Converter

Elektro-pneumatische Marke (GE)

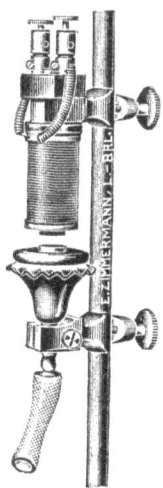

Figure 63. Electropneumatic Converter (Zimmermann, 1912)

The electropneumatic converter transforms electric signals into pneumatic impulses. The instrument combines the principles of the electromagnet and Marey's tambour. When the electromagnet is powered by electric current, it attracts a metal disc fixed to the membrane of the tambour. The movement of the membrane causes a sudden change of pressure in the pneumatic system which corresponds to the size of the electric impulse.

Devices for Research of Visual Perception

Color Mixing Devices

Helmholtz's Color Mixing Apparatus

Spektralfarbenmischapparat nach Helmholtz (GE)

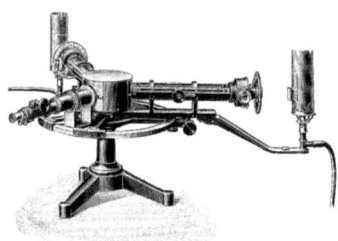

Figure 64. Helmholtz's Color Mixing Apparatus (Zimmermann, 1928)

Helmholtz's apparatus is used for mixing of two homogenous light beams of different wave lengths at any level of intensity. The initial source of white light is provided by a pair of Auer's burners. The light passes through the input optical prisms (which extract the target colors from the white light) into collimators[16] and then into a polished optical prism located in the central oval space of the apparatus. In the prism the light beams are mixed together and focused to the observation tube.

Hering's Optical Color Mixing Apparatus

Farbenmischapparat für farbige Gläser nach Hering (GE)

Figure 65. Hering's Optical Color Mixing Apparatus (Rothe, 1893)

---

16   A collimator is a simple optical device for narrowing a beam of light.

To obtain optimal results, this device must be set in darkened room with a single source of light. The intensity of the light can be regulated by three adjustable milk glass plates. The light enters the device through a triad of colored filters – two on the sides and one at the bottom of the central box. Inside the box there is a system of semi-translucent mirrors which directs the light beams into the output tube. The observer, when looking into the tube, does not see three separate colors, only the resulting compound color. When only two colors are mixed, the redundant light input must be blinded.

Hand Driven Colored Disc[17]

Farbenkreisel für Handbetrieb (GE)

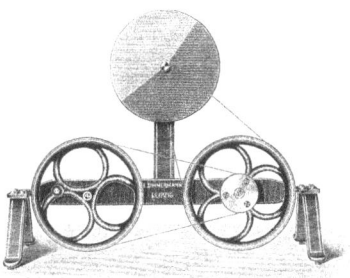

Figure 66. Hand Driven Colored Disc (Zimmermann, n.d.)

 Colored disc rotators used to belong to the basic accessories of psychological laboratories. The principal function of these tools is to rotate discs at high speed causing the colors to blur and mix together. Rotators vary in several ways, including propulsion type, the number of concurrently rotating discs, and the ability to adjust the ratio of colored sector sizes while the device is running. Some specialized devices are also able to rotate two discs in opposing directions.

The earliest rotators used human power and a system of gearing which made it possible to rotate the disc at relatively high revolutions. E.g. Hering's variant of the rotator could reach a speed up to 100 revolutions per second. However, hand-driven devices are generally poor at ensuring invariability, and revolution frequencies might vary depending on the level of the operator's physical exhaustion. This is why the use of such devices was mostly limited to classroom demonstrations. In some cases, the instruments were equipped by flywheels to achieve higher revolutions.

---

17   http://history.psu.cas.cz/machinery/rotating_colored_discs.html

Colored Disc Rotated by Clockwork

Farbenkreisel mit Uhrwerk (GE)

Figure 67. Colored Disc Rotated by Clockwork (Zimmermann, 1912)

In a less physically demanding version, the colored wheels are driven by clockwork rotators. In such cases, the operator's physical exertion is reduced to winding up the mainspring. On the other hand, these devices lack any speed regulators, which means that the revolutions apparently slow down proportionally to the amount of energy released by the mainspring.

Mischotte's Sevenfold Colored Disc

Siebenfacher Farbkreisel nach Mischotte (GE)

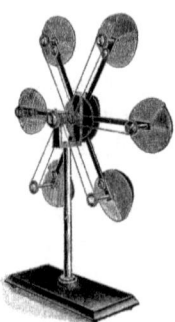

Figure 68. Mischotte's Sevenfold Colored Disc (Zimmermann, 1928)

Rotators with multiple spindles are devices designed to enable rotation of several colored discs at exactly the same speed. Sevenfold rotator has concentrically arranged arms. It can be powered by an engine, and the construction permits rotation frequency up to 2,200 revolutions per minute. There are also other linearly arranged sets driven by a single source which generates a constant number of rotations for all attached discs.

Colored Disc Rotated by Electric Motor

Rotationsapparat für Farbscheiben mit Elektromotor (GE)

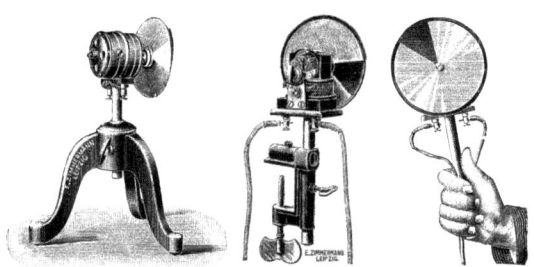

Figure 69. Colored Disc Rotated by Electric Motor (Zimmermann, 1896)

Early laboratories used batteries as a source of electric energy. Hence, rotating colored discs were typically driven by electric motors using low voltage DC power supply (4 – 6 V). The picture 69 demonstrates different alternatives of colored disc fixation – a massive iron table stand, a table clamp, and a movable hand-held variant.

Marbe's Rotator

Rotations-Apparat nach Marbe (GE)

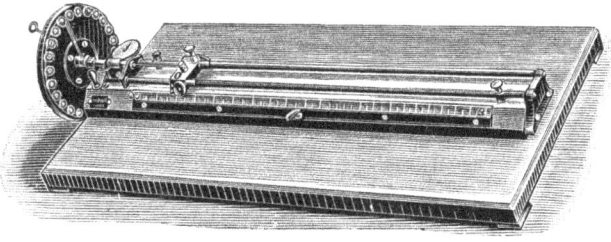

Figure 70. Marbe's Rotator (Zimmermann, 1895a)

Marbe's rotator is one of the earliest models using an internal construction to vary the mutual proportions of colored sector sizes while the disc was in motion. The movement of the control slider along a longitudinal scale is transmitted by means of a string to an internal mechanism which carries out the change in sector proportions of the concentrically arranged colored discs without interfering with their rotation. The scale next to the slider bar indicates the actual sector proportions in arc degrees. This is a considerable improvement over earlier models which had to be adjusted using a protractor. Marbe's rotator is primarily hand-operated, but wiring up an electric motor is also possible.

The designer of the rotator found the mechanism so highly technologically advanced that he even had it patented[18]. Yet, the historical sources indicate that the device did not always function reliably. The internal mechanism contained a gut string which was highly susceptible to over-winding and could break rather easily, catapulting the colored discs throughout the auditorium over the heads of the startled students.

Color Variator (Original Construction)

Farbvariator (Originalkonstruktion) (GE)

Figure 71. Color Variator (Original Construction) (Zimmermann, n.d.)

In spite of being entirely different in terms of construction, this model is functionally equivalent to Marbe's Rotator; it offers continuous variation in color sector size between 0° and 360° without interrupting the device's operation. The adjustments in sector size are carried out by means of a handle attached to a bolt at the end of the instrument. Turning of the bolt moves the adjusting slider. The current size of the sector can be read on the scale next to the slide bar which is calibrated

---

18 D. Reichs-Patent No. 78693 as documented by a note in the Zimmermann Catalogue (1895a).

in tens of degrees while grading by units is indicated around the bolt's circumference. The construction itself is very robust, based on a pair of concentric[19] shafts. The device is always driven by an electric motor which is either connected externally or might be an integrated part of the machine.

Rotator with Split Shaft (Counter-Rotating Discs)

Rotations-Apparat mit Doppelachsen (GE)

Figure 72. Rotator with Split Shaft (Counter-Rotating Discs) (Zimmermann, 1903)

This device has a concentric arrangement meaning that one shaft is embedded in another one. The main advantage of such arrangement is that two concentric discs can be rotated simultaneously at both identical and different speeds and also counter to each other. When another external propulsion component is added, each disc can be set to a different rotation speed.

Consumable Material

Even though colored discs for the rotators could relatively easily be made from one's own sources, in order to maximize comparability of research results from different laboratories researchers preferred to use standard materials. In case ready-made discs were not available, one simply could cut them out of supplied sheets of special colored paper with the help of circular steel templates.

---

19   Concentric arrangement of two shafts means that one shaft is inserted in the other one, sharing the same central axis.

Episcotisters

Aubert's Variable Rotating Sector

Episkotister nach Aubert (GE)

Figure 73. *Aubert's Variable Rotating Sector (Zimmermann, 1912)*

The primary function of episcotisters is to adjust light intensity through a rapid interruption of the light flux. Several experiments using episcotisters were described, for example, by Woodworth and Schlosberg (1959). The model depicted above, Aubert's variable rotating sector, uses a rotating wheel with narrow metal plates arranged in fans. The area obscured by the plates can be varied up the entire 360° when the plates are completely fanned out. Around the edge of the wheel is a groove for a drive belt that can be attached to an engine.

Müller's Episcotister

Zylinderepiskotister nach G. E. Müller (GE)

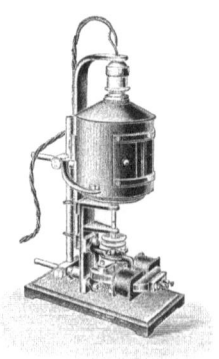

Figure 74. *Müller's Episcotister (Spindler & Hoyer, 1908)*

G. E. Müller's cylindrical episcotister is a more advanced instrument comprising an overshadowing screen, an integrated source of light, and an electric motor which rotates the screen. The surface of the cylinder, spinning around a Nernst lamp[20], is made up of 12 movable sections called selectors. Each selector consists of two connected parts arranged in opposite directions which can be slid into one another. A maximum sliding in of the selectors allows 10/12 of the lamp light to pass through. Mutual shifting of the selectors adjusts the amount of output light to the desired value. The size of selector-covered area is indicated on the outer circular scale. Using this value, the amount of light produced by the device can be calculated, or conversely, the value indicating the target amount of light can be used to calculate the required position of selectors. The description above applies to the inner rotating cylinder which is placed inside a fixed outer cylinder. The outer cylinder has a small opening on one side, covered by a sliding door. The position of the covering determines the size of the illuminated area.

Tachistoscopes

One of the instruments that survived in psychological academe as a useful tool still contributing to the psychological knowledge is the tachistoscope (Zuckerman, 1955; Sperling, 1960; Diehl, McKeever, 1987). The function of a tachistoscope is to enable brief exposure to visual stimuli.

The first attempts to briefly present visual stimuli in a controlled environment can be traced back to the first half of the 19th century, when Dove used an electric spark in his research of stereoscopic perception (Dove, 1841). The spark caused the visual stimulus hidden in a black box to be lit for a short period of time. Around 1850 (Volkmann, 1859), Volkmann constructed an instrument for brief exposure based on a different principle and named it tachistoscope (derived from the Greek word 'tachistos', meaning swiftest). This device replaced spark illumination with simple mechanical uncovering and covering of the stimulus using a horizontally positioned frame drawn by a weight. Later, Volkmann replaced the horizontal construction with a more ergonomically appropriate upright one. Several years later, James McKeen Cattell introduced a tachistoscope enhanced by electromagnetically controlled release of a frame. Cattell (1886a) pointed out the ability of the instrument to accurately measure reaction time and therefore referred to this instrument as a Fall-Chronometer[21]. Apart from this device, a cam-

---

20 An electric bulb producing very bright light.
21 Since we use Wundt's variant of this tachistoscope, we stick to Wundt's terminology (Wundt, 1893a, 1893b) and refer to this device as a fall tachistoscope to maintain terminological consistency.

era-like mechanical shutter was adapted for brief exposure purposes by other researchers (e.g. Dockeray's Camera-Shutter Tachistoscope, Stoelting, 1930, p. 97). After that, a great number of other tachistoscopic instruments were constructed, principally more or less similar to the ones mentioned above. The diversity in tachistoscope construction is well documented by many trade catalogues from different manufacturers of experimental apparatus, collected in the "Virtual laboratory" of the Max Planck Institute for the History of Science in Berlin (Schmidgen, Evans, 2003).

Wundt's Tachistoscope

Tachistoscope nach Wundt (GE)

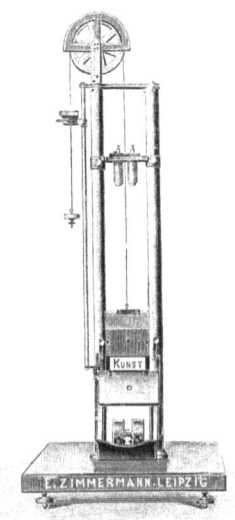

Figure 75. Wundt's Tachistoscope (Zimmermann, 1903)

The instrument can be distinguished by its typical tall and slim construction. It works on the principle of a falling slider which uncovers the stimulus for a very brief time period during the fall. The slider is a flat sheet of metal with an adjustable rectangular window. The exposure time is a function of the length of the slider fall and the vertical dimension of the window. The preparation of every single trial involves several steps: first, computing both the initial vertical position of the slider and the window size in order to set the desired exposition time; second, placing the slider at the top position where it is fixed by a pair of electromagnets; and third, inserting the stimulus card in the holder and masking it with a piece of cloth. When everything is set, the participant is instructed to fix their eyes on the crosshair depicted on the cloth. Then, the administrator interrupts the electric current, which results in the release of the slider. During the fall, the slider dislodges the cloth and for a given time period makes the stimulus visible through the slider window.

Rotary Tachistoscope

Rotations Tachistoskop (GE)

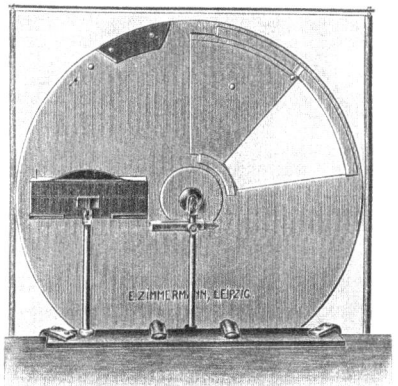

Figure 76. The Back-side of Rotary Tachistoscope (Zimmermann, 1912)

The main component of the rotary tachistoscope is a circular board with a segmental cutout. From the observer's side the device is fully covered by a metal plate with a rectangular window positioned against the stimulus holder. The exposure of the stimulus occurs when the board is released to make a rotational movement around the horizontal axis, during which the cutout reveals the stimulus. The movement is initiated either by a weight hung from pulley fixed to the horizontal axis, or by a flat weight fixed directly to the rotational board. The stimulus is visible only for a very short time period when the cutout is passing by. The duration of the stimulus exposure can be regulated by adjusting the size of the cutout. In contrast with fall tachistoscopes, rotary tachistoscopes produce considerably less disturbing noise. On the other hand, the calculation of the exact exposure time is rather complicated, as it is based on the free fall formula modified for the movement along a circular trajectory (Rameš, 1928).

Netschajeff's Tachistoscope

Tachistoskop nach Netschajeff (GE)

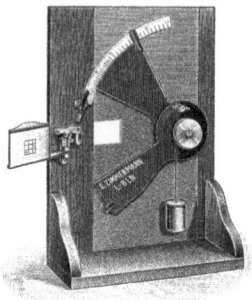

Figure 77. Netschajeff's Tachistoscope (Zimmermann, 1912)

At the back of the instrument there are two blades positioned against each other. In the initial position the bottom blade covers the observation window, behind which there is a holder with the stimulus card. When released, the bottom blade falls down and uncovers the stimulus card until the upper blade covers the window again. The exposure time is set by the angle formed by the blades with the maximum of 65 degrees (150 ms). To prepare another trial, the blades must be manually returned to their initial position and the stimulus card must be replaced. The rotary movement of the blades is facilitated by a weight hung from a pulley fixed to a horizontal axis.

Netschajeff's Tachistoscope, Giese's Construction

Tachistoskop nach Netchajeff mit automatischem Bildvorschub nach Giese (GE)

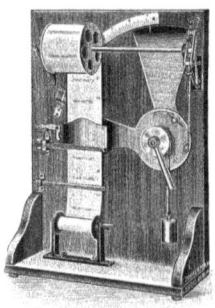

Figure 78. Netschajeff's Tachistoscope, Giese's Construction (Zimmermann, 1928)

This device is a demonstration of the progressive evolution of experimental instrumentation leading to more efficient and smooth laboratory work. This variant of Netchajeff's tachistoscope has replaced the static holder with Giese's automatic stimulus material shifter (Giese, 1925). Individual stimulus sets are written on a paper belt the movement of which is derived from the blades returning into their initial position.

Wirth's and Berliner's Pendulum Tachistoscope

Pendeltachistoskop nach Wirth und Berliner (GE)

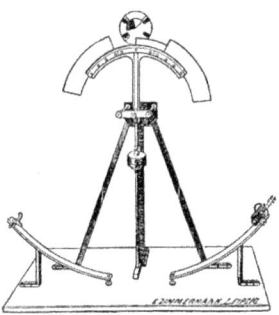

Figure 79. Wirth's and Berliner's Pendulum Tachistoscope (Zimmermann, 1923b)

Wirth's and Berliner's design is based on the swing of a pendulum. The top end of the pendulum carries a holder with two circle sector shields separated by a gap. The size of the gap is adjustable through positioning of the shields. The bottom part of the pendulum is supplied with a sliding weight. Exposure time is set by a combination of two factors – the size of the gap and the position of the weight (Berliner, 1907). To avoid interference of the external environment, the device is equipped with tubular peephole. Between the individual displays the pendulum is held in the left and right dead centers by a pair of electromagnets.

Klemm's Hand Tachistoscope

Handliches Tachistoskop nach Klemm (GE)

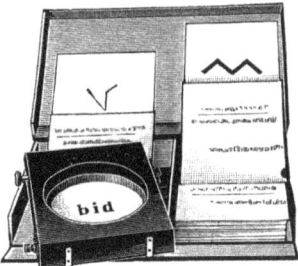

Figure 80. Klemm's Hand Tachistoscope (Zimmermann, 1928)

This pocket-size tachistoscope boasts with dimensions of 25 x 150 x 120 mm (Lanc, 1966). It works with a camera-like mechanical shutter. The control elements – the setting mechanism of the exposition time, the winding crank, and the shutter release – are located on the side of the instrument. When in action, the tachistoscope is put directly over the stimulus and thus needs neither a holder not a feeder.

Tachistoscope with Camera-Like Mechanical Shutter

Tachistoskop mit mechanischem Kameraverschluss (GE)

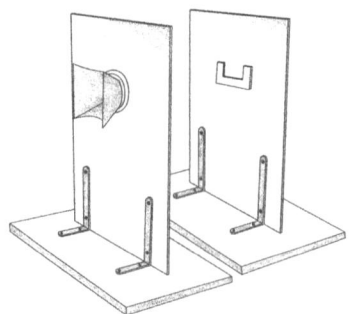

Figure 81. Tachistoscope with Camera-Like Mechanical Shutter

This device uses a photographic shutter with adjustable exposure time (1 – 1/50 s). It is also possible to control the aperture size. The stimulus is fixed by a separate holder. For the comfort of the test subject, but also to minimize the influence of potential extraneous variables (i.e. to eliminate cross light and fix the head position), the design enables the adjustment of the tachistoscope's height, and the device is equipped with face-shaped light shields.

Dodge's Mirror Tachistoscope

Spiegel Tachistoskop nach Dodge (GE)

Figure 82. Dodge's Mirror Tachistoscope (Stoelting, 1930)

Dodge's tachistoscope fulfills virtually all demands put on tachistoscopic devices[22] as stated by Wundt (1900): a) it provides exposure time brief enough to prevent eye movement and attention shift; b) it has the fixation problem resolved by providing a fixation point to focus on in the same place where stimuli would appear; c) the stimulus is presented all at once or with minimized delay between the individual elements of the stimulus; and d) the exposure of the stimulus is not accompanied by a sudden change in brightness of the scene and the induction of an afterimage is sufficiently prevented.

The device works on the principle of a one-way/two-way mirror and alternating lighting of two separate areas. Before the exposure, the stimulus card is inserted into the holder in a darkened rear area of the instrument. At this moment, the test subject cannot see the stimuli but they can see an image of the fixation point from the illuminated right area on a diagonally positioned one-way/two-way mirror. The fixation point is in the same visual distance from the observer as the stimulus card. When the rear area is illuminated and the right area is darkened, the observer can see the stimulus card through the mirror. To minimize the influence of potential extraneous variables, the instrument is equipped with face-shaped light shields.

---

22   Further discussion of this issue and experimental comparison of different tachistoscopes can be found in Voboril, Jelínek, Květon (in press).

Originally, Dodge's tachistoscope used a rotary tachistoscope-like mechanism to generate light flashes (Dodge, 1907). Later models were equipped with lighting fixtures (bulbs or discharge lamps) with short start-up time and minimal afterglow.

Perimeters

Perimeters are devices used mainly for the measurement of visual field limits. The testing is always performed on one eye while the other eye is covered. The test subject is asked to continually fixate a point located on the linear axis in front of them. The movement of a slider along the perimeter's arc helps to determine the position indicated by the test subject as the limit spot where the fixation point can still be detected. Perimeters were also used, for example, in experiments testing reaction time to stimuli presented in the visual periphery.

Wundt's Perimeter

Perimeter nach Wundt (GE)

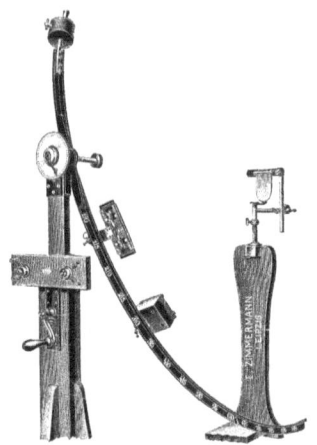

Figure 83. Wundt's Perimeter (Zimmermann, 1903)

Wundt's perimeter is composed of two stands. While the first one provides head fixation with an eye-blinder, the second one carries a rotational quarter arc. The 108 cm long arm has different kinds of sliders attached to it, depending on the type of measurement or experiment. The arc can be turned to adjust its angular position indicated on a scale. The height of the arc's central hollow pivot is adjusted to match the eye position of the test subject. Throughout the testing, the eye has to remain visible through the pivot in the center of the aperture, which serves as the fixation point. When measurements are taken in the dark, the fixation point can be illuminated, while the arc arm carries a slider equipped with a light source and a color filter holder.

Various accessories can be attached to arc sliders such as colored discs, electric lamps with replaceable filters, etc. For example the arc can carry a bulb shining through a glass container filled with a colored fluid serves as a color filter. The advantage of this arrangement is that the desired color hue can be achieved by adding a pre-measured amount of pigment.

Förster's Perimeter

Perimeter nach Förster (GE)

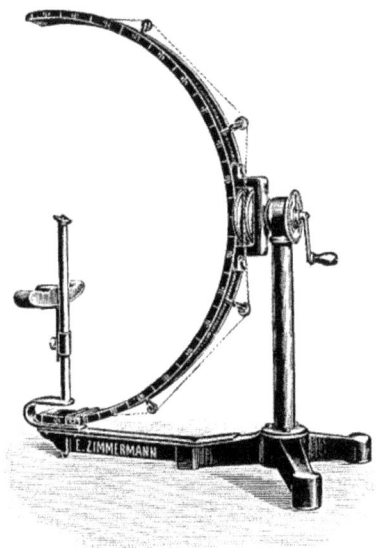

Figure 84. Förster's Perimeter (Zimmermann, 1922a)

In contrast to Wundt's perimeter, where sliders are moved by direct manipulation, in Förster's perimeter the movement is carried out through a set of strings and gears leading from a manually operated handle. The stimulus is attached to the slider, and the turning of the handle moves it along the entire length of a semicircular arc. The size of the resulting angle can be determined by looking at the scale indicating the number of arc degrees.

Hardy's Self Recording Perimeter

Selbstregistrierendes Perimeter nach Hardy (GE)

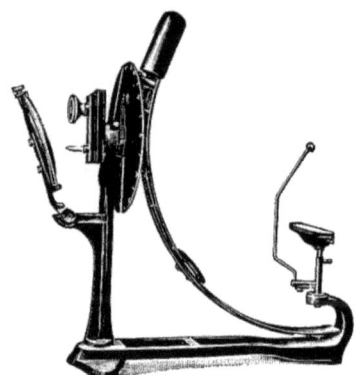

Figure 85. Hardy's Self Recording Perimeter (Zimmermann, 1928)

The arguably most advanced device in this category for the given period is Hardy's perimeter. The main advantage of this instrument is automatic recording of the values measured. The balanced semicircular arc is equipped with a moving object-carrier for exchangeable discs of five different colors (white, yellow, green, red and blue) and six sizes (1, 2, 5, 10, 15 and 20 mm). As soon as the subject identifies the point of their visual field limit, they are supposed to pull a lever of a registering mechanism. The mechanism marks the information about the current angle of the arc and the respective visual field limit by pressing a recording chart against a marking spike.

Other Equipment

Wundt's Ophtalmotrope for Demonstrating the Actions of the Muscles of the Eyeball

Demonstrations-Ophthalmotrop nach Wundt (GE)

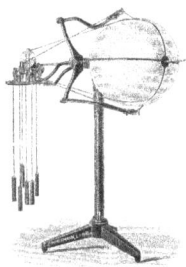

Figure 86. Wundt's Ophtalmotrope for Demonstrating the Actions of the Muscles of the Eyeball (Zimmermann, 1922a)

This tool was used for demonstrations of movements of extraocular muscles. The rod inserted in the center of the ball represents the visual axis and is used for moving the model's position. When turned in particular direction, the activity of individual eye muscles is clearly visible. Six strings, representing the six muscles of the eyeball, attach to the points corresponding to the muscles' insertion spots. The hollow metal ball – a model of the eyeball – has a diameter of 240 mm, and the way it is fastened to the stand enables a 35° rotation in all directions.

Ophtalmotrope (Model of the Muscles of the Eye)

Ophthalmotrop (Augenmuskelmodell) (GE)

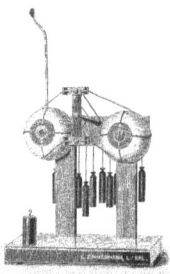

Figure 87. Ophtalmotrope (Model of the Muscles of the Eye) (Zimmermann, 1921a)

A complex model representing both eyes was used to demonstrate the coordinated actions of eye muscles bilaterally, especially during simultaneous eye movements, target fixation, and convergence. The diameter of one eyeball model was 72 mm.

Von Frey's Optical Bench

Optische Bank nach von Frey (GE)

Figure 88. Von Frey's Optical Bench (Zimmermann, 1904)

Experiments with light were conducted using von Frey's experimental set. Optical elements can be attached to a 125 cm long prismatic rail, creating various optical configurations as demanded by the experiment. The set includes frames for opaque glass plates or mirrors, a simple and a double lens holder, tinted filters, an iris, a shield with four extensions, and a fixation cross and arrow.

Spectrometric Apparatus

Spektrometrischer Apparat (GE)

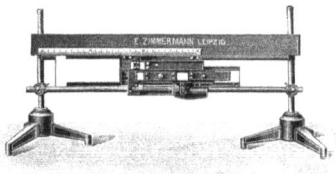

Figure 89. Spectrometric Apparatus (Zimmermann, 1912)

Spectrometers are used for spectral analysis of light. They are able to determine the borders of pure spectral colors (in nanometres) as well as to estimate the relation of a particular color to the Frauenhofer lines[23]. Spectrometers were also used to compare the quality of light produced by laboratory light sources to that of the natural daylight.

---

23   Frauenhofer lines are marked absorption lines found in the optical spectrums of stars described and located in the optical spectrum of the Sun by J. von Frauenhofer in 1814.

Devices for Research of Tactual Perception

Tactual devices were used in research focused on the processing of stimuli registered by the body surface. They were broadly used in psychophysical experiments in the three main areas of perception research – absolute thresholds, discrimination thresholds, and scaling.

Von Frey-Style Temperature Point

Heizspitze nach von Frey (GE)

Figure 90. Von Frey-Style Temperature Point (Zimmermann, 1923c)

Von Frey's temperature point is able to administer stimuli of an exact temperature to a specific spot on the human body. The sensory stimulus is provided by a replaceable contact of various shapes (cone, spherical, or flat). The contact is tempered by the liquid flowing through an attached tube. The temperature of the liquid is controlled by means of an integrated thermometer.

Von Frey's Hair Aesthesiometer

Haar-Ästhesiometer nach von Frey (GE)

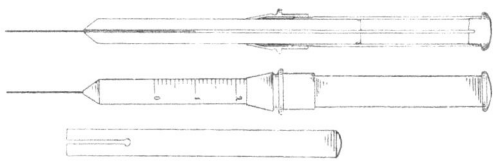

Figure 91. Von Frey's Hair Aesthesiometer (Zimmermann, 1923b)

Von Frey's aesthesiometer is a device for the examination and identification of sensory spots on the human body. It is able to produce an exact degree of pressure on a small area of the skin. The essential part of the device is represented by a hair with one end fixed inside a telescopic tube. The length of the free end of the hair can be telescopically adjusted and checked on the inscribed scale. During an experimental trial, the free end of the hair is pressed against the skin with an increasing force until the hair starts to bow. In the calibration process the exact level of pressure needed to bow the hair is determined using laboratory scales. To ensure comparability of results, the obtained measure is routinely converted into newtons per square millimeter (Woodworth, Schlosberg, 1959).

Spearman's Aesthesiometer

Ästhesiometer nach Spearman (GE)

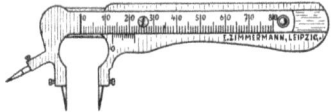

Figure 92. Spearman's Aesthesiometer (Spindler & Hoyer, 1908)

A simple slide caliper with a pair of measuring spikes and one additional checking spike is used to identify the closest distance of two spots on the skin at which the test subject can still differentiate between the two spots. The scale of Spearman's aesthesiometer provides the accuracy at the level of 0.1 mm. The auxiliary third spike can be used to verify the truthfulness of test subject's responses. In the test situation, the respondent can be stimulated at irregular intervals by a single spike without the need to use another tool or to readjust the measurement spike pair.

Ebbinghaus' Aesthesiometer

Ästhesiometer nach Ebbinghaus (GE)

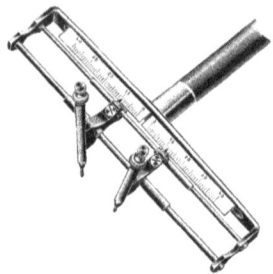

Figure 93. Ebbinghaus' Aesthesiometer (Zimmermann, 1903)

In case of Ebbinghaus' aesthesiometer the stimuli are administered via two ivory spikes. The spikes protrude from metal tubes containing hidden springs which press against the spikes. The tension of the springs can be adjusted by micrometric screws. During the experimental trial the researcher places the device onto the selected spot and pushes it by an intensity which forces the spikes to partly (up to lines marked on the spikes) retract into the tubes. The measurement range of this device is between 0 – 80 millimeters.

Von Frey's Electromagnetic Stimulating Lever

Elektromagnetischer Reizhebel nach von Frey (GE)

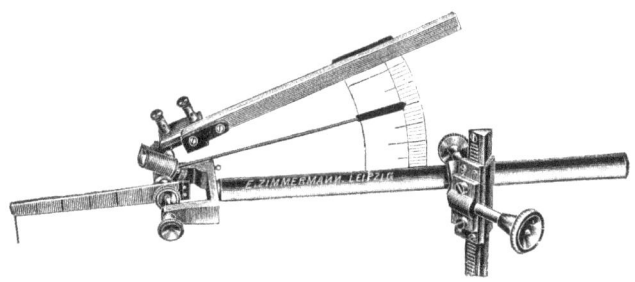

Figure 94. Von Frey's Electromagnetic Stimulating Lever (Zimmermann, 1903)

Automatized von Frey's stimulator is based on electromagnetically induced leverage. The main component of the instrument is a wooden lever with a bristle at the longer end and a metal anchor at the opposite shorter end. The lever is fixed to a holder. The axis of the lever also carries a pole holding the electromagnet and a measurement scale. The scale indicator is attached to the wooden lever. When powered, the electromagnet attracts the anchor and the bristle pushes against the skin. A closer or farther placement of the electromagnet determines the pressure force. The device holder is mounted on a prismatic stand with a side rack ridge to secure a stabilized vertical position. In certain experimental situations it was needed to move the system horizontally to another position in order to reach a different part of test subject's body. For this purpose, the stand was placed on a glass desk powdered with soapstone to make to movement easier.

Von Frey's Apparatus for Measuring Threshold Value of Pressure Sensitivity

Schwellenwage nach von Frey (GE)

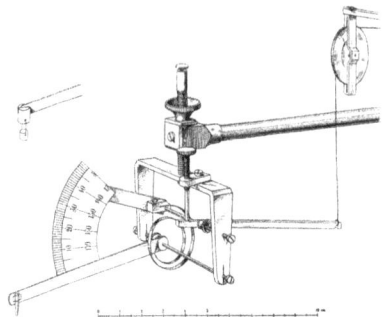

Figure 95. Von Frey's Apparatus for Measuring Threshold Value of Pressure Sensitivity (Zimmermann, 1923b)

In principle, the instrument consists of two levers mounted on two separate axes, interconnected by a clock spring. The pressure of the contact spike at the end of the output lever is produced by pulling the string tied to the input lever. The force applied to the string is transferred between the levers through spring gearing, resulting in the fact that the output force is considerably weakened in comparison with the input force. The contact spike can be replaced with a contact weight which can apply pressure force up to the maximum determined by its mass. The pressure force can be applied all at once by using a weight, or it can be applied gradually, e.g. by slowly adding water drops into a cup attached to the string.

Wundt's Demonstration Aesthesiometer

Demonstrations-Ästhesiometer nach Wundt (GE)

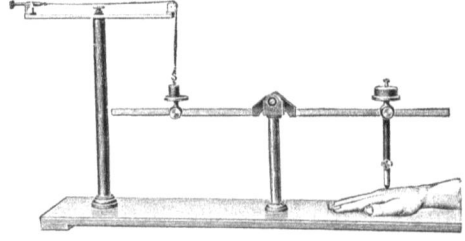

Figure 96. Wundt's Demonstration Aesthesiometer (Zimmermann, 1912)

Wundt's variant of the aesthesiometer is intended for demonstration purposes and thanks to its transparent design and substantial size it well suited for the use in large lecture halls. The device does not provide any readable data. Both parts of the prismatic lever are equipped with sliding cups with weights. Under the cup on the right there is a pole with a vertically adjustable wooden peg. Before starting the trial, the lever is balanced. Administration of stimuli is then carried out by lifting the left weight using a micrometrically operated string.

Stratton-Style Balance for Pressure (Wundt's Aerometer)

Druckwage nach Stratton (In dieser Form nach Wundt) (GE)

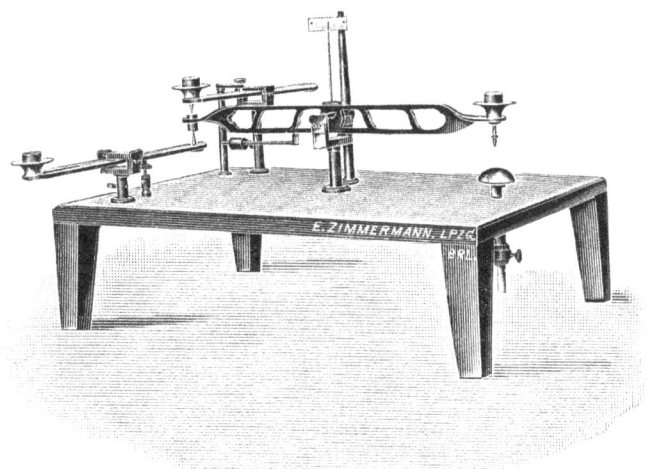

Figure 97. Stratton-Style Balance for Pressure (Zimmermann, 1912)

This instrument consists of a system of three interconnected balances. The central balance is equipped with a contact spike and a weight on one side. The other side carries a sliding weight to keep the initial equilibrium state. The other two auxiliary balances with two identical weights support the equilibrium of the whole system. Applying additional weights to the auxiliary balances disrupts the system's equilibrium and thus increases or decreases the output pressure force. The instrument is also supplied with a measurement scale.

Weights of different masses (0.5, 1, 2, 3, 4, 10, 20, 50, 100, 150, and 200 g) are used for adjusting the pressure force. The weights are shaped to fit precisely in the middle of the balance pans to avoid measurement inaccuracies.

Instruments Used for Study of Hearing

This chapter introduces instruments that were used in research on hearing. Some of them measure objective, i.e. physiological, aspects of hearing (threshold, range, and acuity of auditory perception), while the other ones are specialized for the measurement of subjective variables such as ratings of esthetical quality of consonances, chords, or even metronome ticking.

Hammering Devices

This type of acoustic instruments produces sound by hitting two objects made of high-hardness material against each other. Individual devices vary in the type of material used as well as the principle of operation.

Drop Phonometer

Fallphonometer (GE)

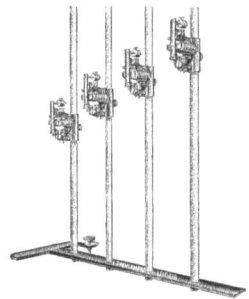

Figure 98. Drop Phonometer (Zimmermann, 1912)

Drop phonometer produces sound by dropping a small metal ball on a hard surface. The same simple principle is shared by a variety of phonometers, e.g. variants designed by Specht, Krueger, Moede, or Lehmann. The main differences consist either in the number of sliding bars, i.e. the number of drops during a single trial, or in the material of the hitting surface (Specht's phonometer, for example, uses an ivory plate).

Each of the four bars is graduated in millimeters and carries a sliding electromagnetic steel-ball holder. When electric current flowing through the holder is interrupted, the ball is released and dropped in a free fall onto an ebony plank. The intensity of the sound produced by the impact exactly corresponds to the height from which the ball is dropped. The complete set also includes a padded box for catching balls rebounding from the plank which would otherwise disrupt the experiment by further bounces.

Zoth's Instrument for Testing Acutement of Hearing[24]

Hörschärfprüfer nach Zoth (GE)

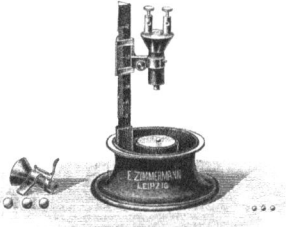

Figure 99. Zoth's Instrument for Testing Acutement of Hearing (Zimmermann, 1903)

 Despite its rather tortuous name, in terms of construction, this instrument belongs to the same category as the drop phonometer. Apparently a tool for the measurement of hearing thresholds, the instrument consists of a vertical bar and a slider used for dropping steel balls of different sizes (diameters of 3.2, 6.4 and 9.6 mm) on a circular steel surface. The impact of steel on steel produces a substantially clear and sharp sound.

Politzer's Acoumeter

Gehörmesser (Akumeter) nach Politzer (GE)

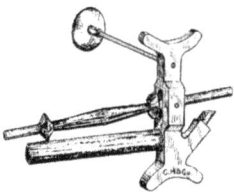

Figure 100. Politzer's Acoumeter (Stoelting, 1930)

This simple tool operated by one hand is able to produce a constant sound stimulus. To work properly, the acoumeter has to be gripped between the thumb and

---

24   http://history.psu.cas.cz/machinery/zoth_hearing_tester.html

the middle finger while the forefinger presses a small lever (the shaped bar in the middle) to its full reach. When the lever is released, the hammer hits the acoumeter's hollow rod, producing a sound of certain intensity. In order to achieve complete invariability and accuracy in the perceived sound intensity, each acoumeter is supplied with a small extension serving to keep the distance from the subject's ear constant.

Sound Pendulums[25]

Schallpendel (GE)

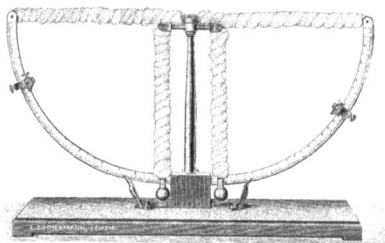

Figure 101. Sound Pendulums (Zimmermann, 1912)

The function of a double-armed sound pendulum is to produce two subsequent sounds of adjustable intensities. The two pendulums can be set at different heights, allowing presentation of sound stimuli of different, pre-determined intensities shortly after each other. The central pillar carries a construction with two movable cord-wrapped pendulums terminating in two ebonite[26] balls. Each quadrant, delineating the pendulum's trajectory, is graduated in arc angles and supplied with a single slider fixed by a bolt. The position of the slider determines the angle from which the pendulum will be swung. The lower part of the instrument contains stops preventing the pendulum from rebounding and causing another impact. Earlier models of the sound pendulum were used without muffling wrappings. Later on, however, in order to reduce resonance and improve the quality of the output sound, the arms of the pendulums were usually covered in dampening material. Various materials other than the ones described above were used in the construction of pendulums. For example, Spindler & Hoyer Company (1908, 1921) used a combination of ebony (ball) and steel (hitting block). Both Zimmermann (1928) and Stoelting (1930), on the other hand, chose ebonite balls and wooden blocks.

---

25 http://history.psu.cas.cz/machinery/sound_pendulums.html
26 Ebonite is natural or synthetic rubber with high sulphur content; hard black material.

Electromagnetic Sound Hammer[27]

Elektromagnetischer Schallhammer (GE)

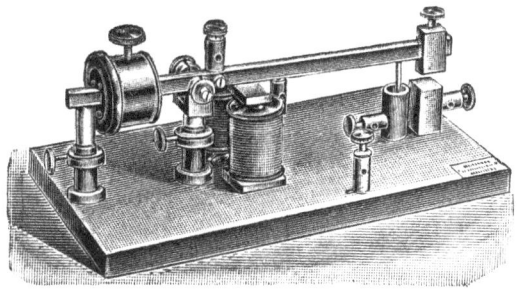

Figure 102. Electromagnetic Sound Hammer (Spindler & Hoyer, 1908)

 When the experiment required that the acoustic instrument be controlled by electric current, this purpose was served by the electromagnetic sound hammer. The main part of the apparatus consists of a piece of hammer-shaped iron attached at the end of a long prismatic arm and a steel cylinder placed against the hammer. When the instrument's electromagnets are connected to electric current, the arm is rapidly drawn towards them and the hammer hits the cylinder, producing a brief and sharp metallic sound. In the most elaborated variant of the instrument an adjustable upper stop enables setting the height from which the hammer falls on the anvil.

A significant advantage of the electromagnetic sound hammer is the possibility to connect another electrical circuit (e.g. switching on a chronoscope in the moment of the clang). This can be done in two different ways. In one version the current flows directly through the arm, the hammer and the steel cylinder (anvil). In the other case the current is passed through cups with mercury in which the contacts attached to the hammer's arm are dipped.

Wind Instruments

A large group of acoustic instruments operates on the principle of air power. The devices in this category have undergone substantial development, starting from the simplest whistles and human lungs up to complex mechanisms driven by bellows and compressors.

---

27 http://history.psu.cas.cz/machinery/electromagnetic_sound_hammer.html

Wooden Whistle

Wooden Whistle (GE)

Figure 103. Wooden Whistle (Helmholtz, 1870)

A very simple acoustic tool is a whistle made of lime wood, resembling of a miniature of the organ pipe. Some types are supplemented with a wooden sliding plunger and a musical scale. The movement of the slide along the scale creates an air column which gives rise to a particular note.

Hornbostel's Travelling Tonometer[28]

Reisetonometer nach Hornbostel (GE)

Figure 104. Hornbostel's Travelling Tonometer (Zimmermann, 1912)

 Travelling tonometer, a portable tuning apparatus, is able to produce up to three consonant notes. The tonometer set consists of three pitch pipes and a middle piece which condenses and collects excessive moisture contained in the breath. The middle piece can be connected to one, two, or all three pitch pipes. All of the pipes are supplied with a diatonic scale. The third one also provides information about the oscillation frequency in the range between 350 – 700 Hz.

---

28   http://history.psu.cas.cz/machinery/hornbostel_travelling_tonometer.html

Galton Whistle

Galton-Pfeifchen (GE)

Figure 105. Galton whistle (Spindler & Hoyer, 1908)

Galton whistle produces high notes by generating air column vibrations between a round flat surface and the air stream running perpendicularly to it through a small tube of the same diameter. The air stream is produced by squeezing a rubber ball at the end of the tube. The sound pitch depends on the distance between the surface and the pipe, which is adjustable. In Edelmann's[29] variant of Galton whistle (see picture 105), unlike the original model, both parts of the whistle are moveable and their mutual distance can be determined with accuracy of 0.1 mm.

Tone Box[30]

Tonmesser nach Appunn (GE)

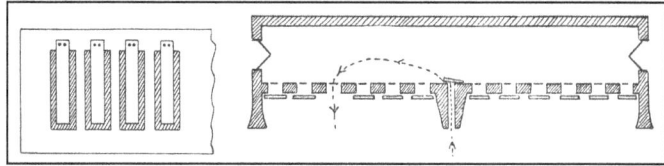

Figure 106. Tone Box (Spindler & Hoyer, 1908)

The tone box[31] works on the principle of an accordion. The bottom of the box contains rectangular openings with metal reeds hitched on the lower side (see picture 106). Under each reed there is a sliding valve. The control mechanism of each valve terminates on the front board of the box. When air passes over the reeds, they oscillate in a particular frequency, producing a sound. The number of valves which can

---

29 Edelmann was a technician working in Munich (Feldmann, 1995)
30 http://history.psu.cas.cz/machinery/tone_box.html
31 The original design of the tone box is attributed to Appunn (Spindler & Hoyer, 1921). The listing of the Leipzig Laboratory equipment (Wundt, 1909) also contains a note on reed tonometers produced by G. & A. Appunn's workshop in Hanau.

be opened simultaneously, as well as the number of simultaneously played sounds, is only limited by the level of air pressure contained in the set. The air is driven from the compressor to the hollow interior of the box, where the excess pressure lifts the upper lid imperviously connected to the body of the box by a piece of leather. The counter pressure of the lid helps to achieve air pressure constancy. These instruments are often also referred to as harmonic tone boxes, or modulometers. They can be used as modulometers because the reeds are able to sustain their tuning for a long time and thus provide a good reference criterion for other acoustic devices.

Bottle Organ

Flaschen-Orgel (GE)

Figure 107. Single Bottle Whistle (Helmholtz, 1870)

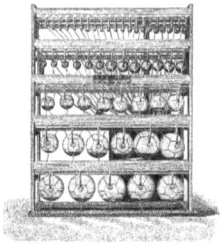

Figure 108. Bottle Organ (Spindler & Hoyer, 1908)

The basic mechanism of the following instrument, in which glass bottles of various sizes are used to achieve different sounds, can be traced back to Helmhotz (1870). A flattened gutta-percha[32] tube (a mouthpiece) is attached to the mouth of the bottle. When the air flows from the compressor through the flat opening of the tube, a sound similar to the vowel 'u' is produced. The sound is very clear, accom-

---

32   Gutta-percha is elastic material made from the milky sap of certain – especially tropical – types of trees. The properties of the material are similar to those of natural rubber.

panied only by very soft murmur of the air stream. The bottles are tuned by means of adding or removing water, which determines the height of the air column inside the bottle.

The same principle is the basis of an instrument called "bottle organ", constructed in the Berlin Psychological Institute (Spindler & Hoyer, 1908; Marx, 1913). It is composed of altogether 54 spherical bottles, tempered in a chromatic scale ranging from C to f3, covering 5 most important octaves. The air needed for the apparatus' functioning is driven from the wind chest to the organ manual. When a key is pressed, the air flows through an opened valve and a tube up to the mouth of the corresponding bottle. Tuning is done by means of hot paraffin which solidifies after being poured into the bottle, forming a column of a particular height.

Stern Tone Variator

Tonvariator nach Stern (GE)

Figure 109. Stern Tone Variator (Spindler & Hoyer, 1908)

Stern's tone variator uses the principle of sound produced by a stream of air flowing over a bottle mouth. Its advantage over simple bottle whistle is that the tone pitch can be varied smoothly by changing the bottom level of a cylinder. Inside the cylinder is a piston with a rod which descends to a spiral-shaped cam (the shape creates variable cavity height required for changing the sound pitch). The cam is rotated manually by means of a small wheel and gearing in a ratio of 1:10; the circular plate is graduated, showing sound frequencies. However, as Spindler & Hoyer (1921) point out, these instruments are susceptible to environmental changes and require frequent calibration. The Figure 109 shows a set of three tone variators with the ranges of 300–600, 400–800 and 500–1000 Hz, and a source of air pressure added by G. M. Whipple (1901a,b). A system of valves controls the air flow, directing it towards one or all three variators.

Accessories for Auditory Perception Devices

Air Compressor

Luftkompressor (GE)

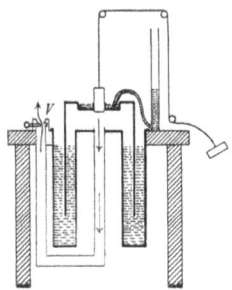

Figure 110. Air Compressor (Spindler & Hoyer, 1908)

All of the above described instruments are highly demanding in terms of uniform air supply. Even the smallest fluctuations would have a negative impact on the sound quality. For this reason, various devices were designed securing the required degree of air compression. One of such compressors is illustrated in the figure 109 showing the compressor connected to the three Stern variators. Figure 110 depicts the principle of the compressor. A cylindrical bell is gradually submerged into a water-filled tank with the open bottom down. The submersion reduces the volume of the bell's cavity with the excessive air escaping – under a constant pressure – through the tube up to the outlet valve V from which it is distributed to the individual instruments. One drawback[33] of such mechanism is quite obvious: When the bell is lifted, the air supply is always interrupted, if only for a short time. A tiny technical refinement solves the less apparent problem of the bell being buoyed up by the water. As the bell is sunk underwater, it is essentially being lifted up with a force proportional to the depth of submersion. This effect is eliminated by providing continuous ballasting of the bell by water: A pipe gradually fills the bowl-shaped upper part of the bell with exactly the same amount of water as that which has been displaced by the bell. For information, the time of the bell's submersion – and hence the time of a constant air pressure supply – necessary to sustain an a1 sound was approximately 45 seconds.

---

33 The issue of air supply interrupting resolves doubled air compressor by Whipple.

Bellows

Faltenbalg (GE)

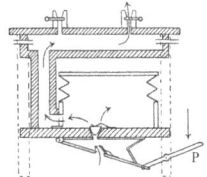

Figure 111. Bellows (Spindler & Hoyer, 1908)

Considerably less sophisticated and less efficient air-pressure devices are various types of bellows – simple, pedal-driven mechanisms (see Figure 111). Pressing the pedal P compresses the bellows, forcing the air through a valve into the air tank. The upper part of the vessel pushes against the incoming air, creating sufficiently steady air pressure which is subsequently delivered to the piping connecting the bellows with acoustic instruments.

Resonators

Resonatoren (GE)

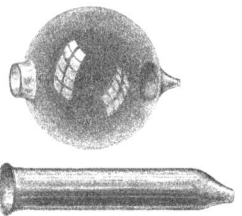

Figure 112. Spherical and Cylindrical Resonators (Helmholtz, 1870)

Resonators are specially designed objects with a high-quality resonance profile working on the principle of acoustic oscillation of a cavity-enclosed environment. The resonator's frequency is determined by its size, cavity shape and the size of the opening (Lanc, 1966). A typical resonator is comprised of a hollow glass or metal sphere or cylinder with two inlets. Whereas the input opening has sharp edges, the output one is rounded, so as to be safely inserted into the ear. Acoustic isolation is enhanced by heated sealing wax applied to the opening shortly before its insertion into the auditory canal. The wax will adjust to the shape of the ear canal, creating a perfectly fitting link between the ear and the resonator which can be used repeatedly if needed (Helmholtz, 1870). Other resonator variants include, for example, models by Koenig or Schaefer, both with cylindrical bodies, enabling continuous adjustment of the inner cavity volume.

Wundt's Sound Interruptor

Schallunterbrecher nach Wundt (GE)

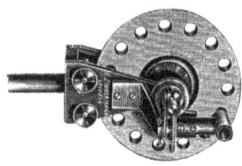

Figure 113. Wundt's Sound Interruptor (Zimmermann, 1912)

In Wundt's variant of sound interruptor, the sound is conducted through a thick-walled rubber tube from the source to the input. The rotating disc contains 15 apertures, alternately covering and uncovering the passage to the output at the other side of the instrument. The apertures can be filled by metal plugs, varying the characteristics of sound passage. The disc is rotated by means of an externally connected electric motor.

Devices for Research of Olfaction and Taste

The issues of human olfaction and taste tend to be rather marginal in the field of psychological research. That is why instruments connected with this area can only be found in the period trade catalogues.

Zwaardemaker's Instrument for Testing Sense of Smell (Olfactometer)

Olfaktometer nach Zwaardemaker (GE)

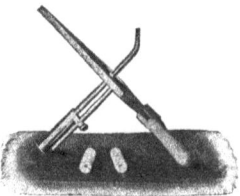

Figure 114. Zwaardemaker's Instrument for Testing Sense of Smell (Zimmermann, 1912)

Olfactometer is a simple instrument used for administering odor stimuli and detecting olfactory thresholds. A kaolin tube impregnated with aromatic substance is placed on a glass tube. The kaolin tube is shielded by a metal casing to avoid interference with external smells. The surrounding air naturally flows through the hole in the back of the metal casing and, aromatized with the substance inside the kaolin tube, finally comes out throughout the glass tube. The concentration of the aroma is controlled by the depth of the glass tube insertion (i.e. reduction or enlargement of the contact surface between the air and the kaolin tube). To reduce the reactivity of the test subject, the mechanism for adjusting the strength of the stimulus is hidden behind a wooden partition.

Taste Stimulators

Geschmack Stimulator (GE)

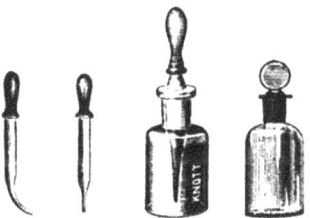

Figure 115. Taste Stimulators (Knott, 1921)

Just as in case of other senses, also in the domain of taste researchers focused widely on perceptual thresholds. For this purpose, stimuli of standardized intensity were produced, mainly in the form of solutions of different concentrations (Bailey, Nichols, 1883). The substances themselves were administered on the tongue of the test subject using a small brush, a glass rod, or a medicine dropper.

Devices for Research of Memory and Learning

Instruments described in this chapter are intended for automatic presentation of visual stimuli in given time intervals. These instruments can be also used for automatic replacement of stimulus material during tachistoscopic experiments.

Rotary Apparatus for Memory Testing Designed by Müller-Pilzecker

Rotations-Apparat für Gedächtnisstudien nach Müller-Pilzecker (GE)

Figure 116. Rotary Apparatus for Memory Testing Designed by Müller-Pilzecker (Zimmermann, 1903)

The mechanical design of this device resembles that of a kymograph. The main component of the apparatus is a horizontally positioned drum with attached stimulus cards. The drum rotates slowly and the observer can see the individual cards through a window with an adjustable vertical dimension. The movement of the drum is driven by spring clockwork connected through a friction gearing mechanism. The speed of the rotation can be regulated by varying the position of a friction wheel on the diameter of the propelling disc and by adjusting the air blades. The instrument is equipped with an inbuilt tachometer. The set was delivered with drums of various sizes. The smoothness of the drum's rotation prevents an all-at-once display of the stimuli.

Ranschburg's Apparatus for Testing Perception, Association, and Memory (Mnemometer)[34]

Apparat zur Untersuchung der Auffassung, Association und des Gedächtnisses nach Ranschburg (Mnemometer) (GE)

Figure 117. Ranschburg's Apparatus for Testing Perception, Association, and Memory (Zimmermann, 1912)

 Ranschburg's apparatus can be used to present various visual stimuli, e.g. words, numerical tasks, colors, or geometrical shapes. The apparatus contains a hidden propelling mechanism consisting of an electromagnet, an anchor, and a cogwheel. Each incoming electric impulse powers the electromagnet. The anchor attracted to the electromagnet elicits a one-cog movement of the wheel (ratchet pawl mechanism). The axis of the cogwheel carries a circular piece of cardboard with the stimulus material. The whole cardboard disc is hidden behind the front panel with an observation window. The disc finishes one revolution after 60 impulses, which is also the maximum number of stimulus material units displayed.

The standard accessories delivered with Ranschburg's apparatus included a metronome with mercury contacts, a telegraph key, and a power source. Depending on the design of the experiment, the controlling impulses are generated either by a metronome set to the required frequency, or manually by pressing a telegraph key.

Apart from the main contacts powering the electromagnet, Ranschburg's mnemometer is supplemented with secondary contacts for connecting additional devices to extend the functionality of the mnemometer. For instance, connecting Hipp's chronoscope and Römer's key to the system allows performing associative experiments with the measurement of reaction time to the stimuli presented by mnemometer.

---

34 http://history.psu.cas.cz/machinery/ranschburg_mnemometer.html

Wirth's Memory Apparatus

Gedächtnisapparat nach Wirth (GE)

Figure 118. Wirth's Memory Apparatus (without front panel) (Zimmermann, 1903). From left to right - disc variant, belt variant.

The device rotates a paper disc with radially arranged stimulus material. The disc is attached to a central wheel with a hanging weight. Two anchors prevent the wheel from rotating until a pair of electromagnets alternately attracts the anchors and thus allows jump shifts of the wheel. The impulses for turning on the electromagnets can be provided by a metronome with mercury contacts.

The disc variant has a limited number of spots for the stimulus units, depending on the number of cogs on the wheel. Therefore, Wirth designed another variant of the device which uses a paper belt as the stimulus medium instead of the disc. Propelling of the device is based on the same principle, but the paper belt is wrapped around the perimeter of a supplementary wheel.

Memory Association Device[35]

Gedächtnisassoziationgerät (GE)

Figure 119. Memory Association Device (Spindler & Hoyer, 1908)

---

35 http://history.psu.cas.cz/machinery/memory_association_device.html

Memory association device is primarily intended for presentation of stimulus pairs. Accordingly, the front panel of the device has two observation windows, adjustable by vertical and horizontal screens. The paper disc with stimulus material is fastened to the main wheel propelled by a hanging weight whose string is wound around the wheel's axis. The wheel is rimmed with 24 protruding, evenly distributed metal pegs. Next to the wheel, there is a horizontally oriented small rotating disc propelled by clockwork. The step-by-step blocking of the metal pegs by the small disc stops the main wheel from rotating. The main wheel can make another move in the rotation when the blocked peg falls through one of the peg-sized cutouts in the small disc. The small disc makes 1 revolution in 4 seconds, and the stimulus exposure time depends on the number of cutouts. The instrument was delivered with a set of small discs with different number of cutouts (1 cut = 4 sec exposure time, 2 cuts = 2 sec, 3 cuts = 4/3 sec, and 4 cuts = 1 sec).

Instruments for the Measurement of Physiological Variables

Due to the limited technological possibilities at the turn of the 20th century, physiological processes such as heart rate, breathing or limb volume changes could only be observed and measured through their external manifestations. In most cases, measured values were recorded by means of a kymograph.

Cardiographs

The function of cardiographs is to obtain a graphical record of the heart's activity over time. The original cardiographs are based on the principle of Marey's tambour and pneumatic transmission of information between a sensor and the recording device. The sensor is typically applied and attached to the spot on the subject's chest where the pulse is most easily palpable. Physical indicators of the pulse are transmitted through a contact button onto the tambour's membrane and further on by pneumatic transfer to the recording device.

Registering Capsule for Marey's Cardiograph

Aufnahmekapsel des Marey'schen Kardiographen (GE)

Figure 120. Registering Capsule for Marey's Cardiograph (Langendorff, 1891)

According to Otto's dictionary (1898), Marey's cardiograph is the oldest instrument of this type. It consists of a bell-shaped chamber which supports a tambour with an internal spring designed to keep the contact button pressed tightly against the subject's chest. A lock-nut on the upper external part of the bell chamber can move the tambour and make very subtle adjustments to its position with respect to the body. Fabric straps attached to the chamber from the outside provide fixation of the sensor to the selected spot on the chest.

Cardiograph According to Burdon-Sanderson

Cardiograph von Burdon-Sanderson (GE)

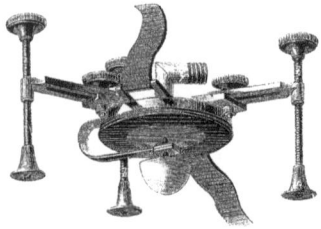

Figure 121. Cardiograph According to Burdon-Sanderson (Cyon, 1876a)

This cardiograph uses the same mechanism of pulse recording as the previous one; the bell chamber, however, has been replaced by three adjustable legs. In comparison with Marey's cardiograph, this construction's props can be better adjusted to fit female body proportions in particular (Zimmermann, 1928). The instrument's position on the body is secured by fabric straps fastened around the subject's chest and neck.

Sanderson's Cardiograph

Cardiograph nach Sanderson (GE)

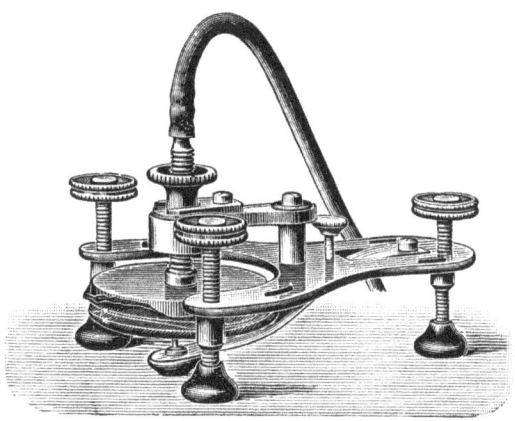

Figure 122. Sanderson's Cardiograph (Zimmermann, 1912)

Another level in the evolution of cardiographs is represented by Sanderson's model which enables finer adjustment regulation in several aspects. The central plate carries three adjustable legs with oval hard-rubber bases which serve to modify the basic distance between the plate and the chest wall. The pressure exerted by the contact button on the chest is regulated by a set screw which controls the tension in the pressure spring. To a certain extent, the position of Marey's tambour can also be varied. Pressure deviations sensed by the contact button are transmitted mechanically through a spherical knuckle joint to the tambour and then further on to the kymograph. The device is fixed on the body by means of straps tied around the chest and neck. After minor modifications, Sanderson's cardiograph can also function as a pneumograph.

Pneumographs

Pneumographs are instruments measuring and recording changes in the volume of chest cavity during inspiration and expiration. Originally, pneumographs were a common part of physiological laboratory equipment, and they were borrowed by psychologists later on. Hence, pneumograph designers were typically physiologists.

Lehmann's Pneumograph

Pneumograph nach Lehmann (GE)

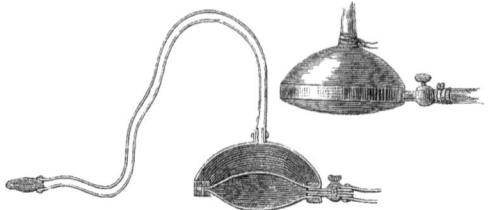

Figure 123. Lehmann's Pneumograph (Cyon, 1876a)

The most remarkable member of this category is Lehmann's pneumograph. Fastened by a string around the subject's chest or abdomen, the instrument transmits chest cavity volume changes to the recorder via an air cushion. In essence, it is a hollow metal capsule closed by two elastic membranes. The feeding tube on the right opens into the space between these two membranes, and is used to blow up the space between the membranes to create air cushion. The output tube on the top leads off the inner cavity of the capsule and pneumatically transmits movements of the air cushion.

Marey's Pneumograph

Pneumograph nach Marey (GE)

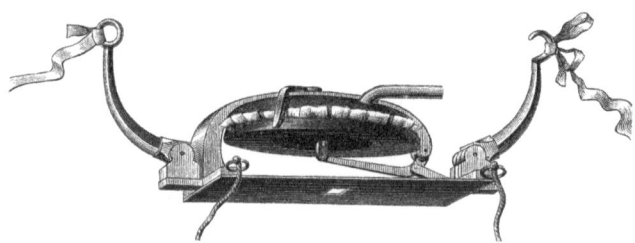

Figure 124. Marey's Pneumograph (Zimmermann, 1903)

Marey's pneumograph is attached to the chest by two fabric straps, while height fixation is performed by means of a supplementary strip fastened around the neck. Changes in chest cavity volume during breathing are transmitted via knuckle joints on the tambour and then pneumatically to the recording device. During expiration, the pneumograph returns to its initial position thanks to an inbuilt flat spring.

Tube Pneumograph

Tube Pneumograph (GE)

The simple sensor of this pneumograph consists of a single rubber tube. The tube is corrugated to make breathing more comfortable. One end of the tube is hermetically sealed; the other carries a holder for the attachment of the output tube. The device can be fastened around the chest or abdomen with the help of two straps. Changes in the chest or abdomen girth during respiration cause deformations in the tube which are subsequently conveyed to the recording device.

Bert's Stethograph

Stethograph nach Bert (GE)

Figure 125. Bert's Stethograph (Cyon, 1876a)

Stetographs are devices used for registering movements of individual points on the chest or abdominal wall. The sensory surface is pressed against the selected spot by means of a spring. The sensor itself is attached to a robust stand with a knuckle joint that enables adjustment and fixation in the desired position. The movements on the sensory disc are transferred to the recorder by means of Marey's tambour and pneumatic transmission.

Bert-Style Cycle Stethograph

Zirkelstethograph nach Bert (GE)

Figure 126. Bert-Style Cycle Stethograph (Cyon, 1876a)

A more recent variant of Bert's stethograph does not require the test subject to remain in a stiff position against the sensor as the earlier model does. Instead, it is secured around the subject's body by means of a clamp mechanism. The clamp device is adjustable in length and allows the sensor to be placed and held anywhere on the chest. Chest movements inside the clamp are transmitted to the tambour and pneumatically to the recorder.

Plethysmographs

Plethysmographs are instruments recording volume changes of the body or individual body parts.

Lehmann-Style Plethysmograph

Plethysmograph nach Lehmann (GE)

Figure 127. Lehmann-Style Plethysmograph (Zimmermann, 1904)

Lehmann's plethysmograph is exclusively used for the measurement of volume changes in the forearm. To ensure that the arm is completely still throughout the experiment while its position remains adjustable for repeated measurements, the instrument is equipped with a movable cushioned elbow rest. The position of the rest can be set according to graduated scale and fixed. The arm-cylinder sensor, made of zinc sheets, is thickly padded from the inside with cotton wool, cloths and leather. Apart from that, it contains a water sack made of fine rubber. When filled with water, the sack occupies the entire space between the arm and the metal cylinder's wall. The water then also essentially pours up into a small glass cylinder supplied with a reduction valve for the attachment of a rubber tube which leads to the recording device. The glass cylinders are replaceable (10 or 25 cm), making it possible to vary the pressure exerted on the forearm. There exists also other pletysmographs that use arm cylinders made of glass, which means that the complete apparatus including suspension and fixings is more clearly visible (e.g. Kronecker's Plethysmograph or Mosso's Plethysmograph).

Manometers

Von Frey's Tonograph

Metall-Tonograph nach von Frey (GE)

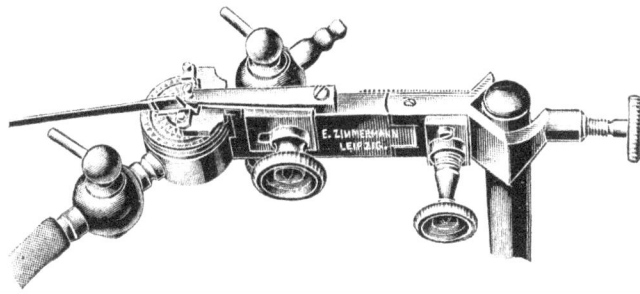

Figure 128. Von Frey's Tonograph (Zimmermann, 1903)

Von Frey's tonograph uses the same principle as a classic pneumatic recording device – pressure in an enclosed space is transmitted to a sensory membrane which responds to the changes and communicates them to the recording stylus. A unique point about von Frey's tonograph, used for the measurement of high blood pressures, is that its shaped membrane is made of a platinum-iridium sheet. Indisputable advantages of this instrument are absolute imperviousness, high durability, resistance to deformations caused by sharp pressure increases, and sensitivity to very subtle pressure changes. Measurement accuracy is even more enhanced by the fact that the lever of the recording stylus is positioned with a couple of steel points in metal sleeves.

Ludwig-Cyon's Mercury Manometer

Quecksilbermanometer nach Ludwig-Cyon (GE)

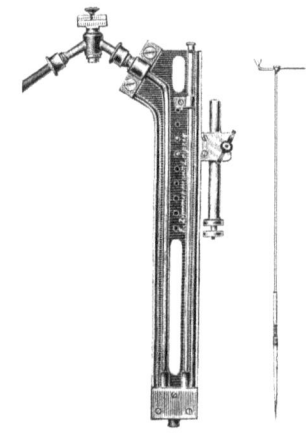

Figure 129. Ludwig-Cyon's Mercury Manometer (Zimmermann, 1903)

Ludwig-Cyon's manometer is mainly used for measurement of blood pressure. If pressure in the incoming tube on the left is increased, the level of mercury in the right glass pipe also rises, lifting up a float. The movement of the float is then transmitted via a steel needle to the glass pipette located at its upper end. The pipette, filled with ink, touches the sheet of the recorder, drawing a curve indicating blood pressure variations.

An instrument principally identical to Ludwig-Cyon's manometer is Böhm's manometer. The difference is that the latter only uses a single U-shaped pipe with a side inlet of the supply tube.

Sphygmographs

Sphygmographs are devices which, when applied to an artery, are able to provide a graphical recording of the pulse waves reflecting heart activity.

Marey-Style Transmitted Sphygmograph

Transmissions-Sphygmograph nach Marey (GE)

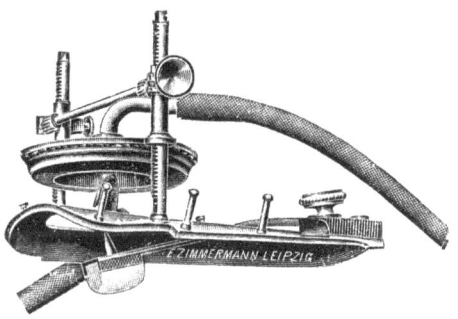

Figure 130. Marey-Style Transmitted Sphygmograph (Zimmermann, 1903)

After the device is fastened to the inner forearm, the contact button is pressed to the pulse point, i.e. the spot where the pulse is most easily palpable. The movement is mechanical, transmitted via a flexible ball pivot to the membrane of Marey's tambour, and then pneumatically through a rubber tube to the stylus of an externally connected kymograph.

Von Frey-Style Sphygmograph

Sphygmograph nach von Frey (GE)

Figure 131. Von Frey-Style Sphygmograph (Zimmermann, 1895b)

The basic construction element of von Frey's sphygmograph is a skid-like plate at the bottom which is fastened onto the forearm by means of a fabric strip. The plate bears the sphygmograph itself; its position on the plate is adjustable, allowing the contact button to be moved to a spot where the pulse can be most clearly detected. A steady pressure of the button onto the selected spot is secured by a flat spring. The pulse is conveyed mechanically from the button directly to the stylus touching the recording drum which rotates by means of its own driving mechanism. In the lower part of the drum the Figure 131 also shows a Jaquet chronograph constructed exclusively for registering a time axis with the frequency of 1/5 s.

After the recording drum and the chronograph are removed, and mechanical transmission is replaced with pneumatic transmission, we obtain a lightweight variant of the same instrument where measured variables are communicated to a kymograph, which enables parallel recording of several types of data.

Recording Apparatus for Pulse etc.

Registrierapparat für Pulsversuche usw. (GE)

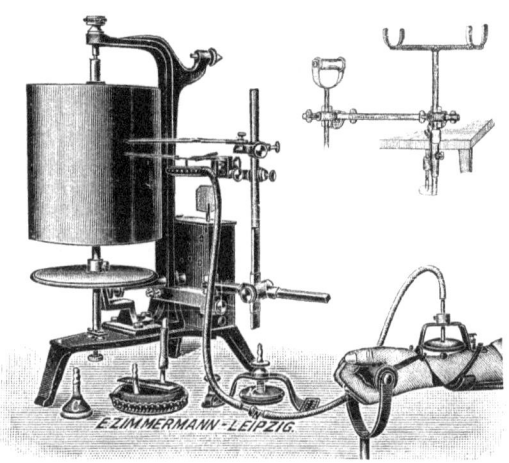

Figure 132. Recording Apparatus for Pulse etc. (Zimmermann, 1928)

The complex apparatus for the recording of pulse shown in the picture above is composed of a kymograph, registration device, linking components, arm rest, and sensors. The sensors include simple Marey's tambour, Lehmann's pneumograph, and a sphygmograph. Out of the set depicted above, Lehmann's sphygmograph is of particular interest. It consists of a brass bracket carrying a Marey's tambour and a contact button attached to the forearm by means of a fabric tape. The vertical position of both the tambour and the button with respect to the arm is adjustable. The movements of the contact button reflecting the pulse are conveyed to the tambour's membrane and then pneumatically to the recording device.

Devices for Measurement of Muscle Characteristics

Tremometers

Tremometers are devices used to record trembling of fingers or other body parts.

Moede's Tremometer

Tremometer nach Moede (GE)

Figure 133. Moede's Tremometer (Zimmermann, 1928)

Moede's tremometer is designed to measure the tremor of the hand. The front panel contains milled-out tracks and holes of different shapes and sizes. The test subject is instructed to move a metal stick along one of the tracks or to hold the stick in one of the holes without touching the edges. Any contact between the stick and the metal material of the front panel closes the electric circuit, sounds a bell, and produces a mark on an electromagnetic kymograph connected to the set.

An interesting modification of this device (resembling some of today's simple computer games) features a rotating brass drum instead of a static desk. A winding track is milled out in the drum, and the test subject attempts to keep a metal stick within the track while the drum is rotated.

Sommer's Apparatus for Analyzing the Motions of the Hand in Three Dimensions

Apparat zur dreidimensionalen Analyse von Bewegungen an den Händen nach Sommer (GE)

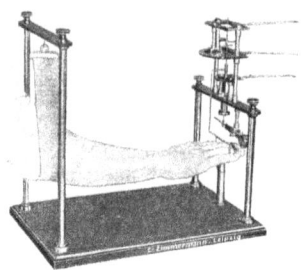

Figure 134. Sommer's Apparatus (Zimmermann, 1912)

Sommer's apparatus provides complex data for a detailed analysis of finger movement. The hand of test subject is freely suspended and the fingers are connected with a recording mechanism through a system of connecting rods. The finger movements in any direction are transferred to the corresponding marker which produces a recording on the kymograph's drum.

Ergographs

Ergographs are devices used for continuous examination and recording of muscle performance.

Mosso's Ergograph

Ergograph nach Mosso (GE)

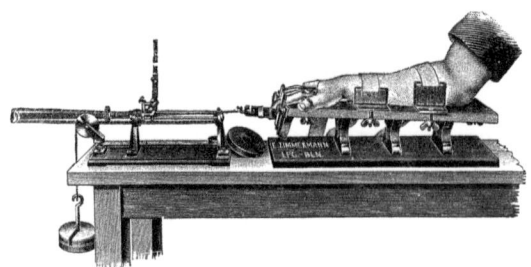

Figure 135. Mosso's Ergograph (Spindler & Hoyer, 1908)

This ergograph belongs to the group of finger ergographs, which measure the performance of individual fingers. It consists of two parts: a comfortable and sizable upholstered armrest and a registration device. The whole forearm is firmly fastened in the armrest so that the tested finger can freely bend. Before the beginning of an experimental trial the finger is fitted into metal cap connected with a hanging weight. The test subject is instructed to pull and release the weight. The pull movement is transferred to a 1 m recording loop, so that after the trial it is possible to read the total distance of the weight's upward movement. The marker attached to the string connecting the cap with the weight transforms the movements into a shaped curve on the kymograph's drum.

Dubois' Ergograph

Ergograph nach Dubois (GE)

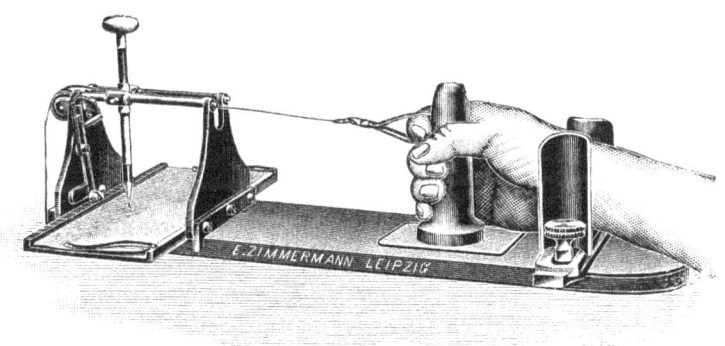

Figure 136. Dubois' Ergograph (Zimmermann, 1905)

During the experimental trial, the test subject holds an ergonomically shaped wooden pin to keep the hand motionless. With a finger hooked in a leather loop he/she repeatedly pulls a string with a weight hanging over a pulley. The space between the loop and the pulley there is occupied by a simple registration device consisting of a marker connected to a string and a slide desk with millimeter paper. The desk is automatically shifted every time the finger is released. Due to the limited space available for the recording medium, the weights used in the experiments were considerably heavy to reach the critical muscle fatigue in several pulls. This limitation has been overcome in the paper-belt variant of the device. Another variant uses a kymograph instead of an inbuilt recording medium and thus provides continuous recording of finger movements over time.

Meumann-Style Ergograph

Ergograph nach Meumann (GE)

Figure 137. Meumann-Style Ergograph (Zimmermann, 1904)

The Meumann's ergograph features an advanced and elaborated mechanism for hand fixation. It consists of an ergonomically bent pad, a forearm holder, a wrist holder, and a complete set of finger holders. All of the holders are graduated to enable exact replication of the hand fixation in subsequent experiments with the same person. The front side of the pad contains a cutout for free movement of the examined finger. The finger is fastened in an upholstered metal cap with a string connected to a weight hanging over a wheel mechanism. When pulling the string, the force must overcome the resistance of the hanging weight. The mechanism is equipped with distance measurement wheel (measuring the overall distance of the pull). The device does not provide any graphical registration of the measurement outputs.

During long-term experiments an additional revolution counter can be attached. The counter, with a maximum of 40 revs, enables the measurement of a total distance up to 10 m (with the wheel perimeter of 250 mm).

Dynamometers

Dynamometers are used for the assessment of static muscle power of various muscle groups. These devices were manufactured in several variants which were all based on the same principle of applying pressure against a spring. Dynamometers usually provide two basic outputs: the levels of immediate and maximum force. The mechanism consists of a measurement scale and two pointers. The immediate force pointer pushes the maximum force pointer into its maximum deviation. As the immediate force pointer returns to its initial position after the mechanism is released, the maximum pointer stays in the position of maximum deviation.

Figure 138. Dynamometers (Zimmermann, 1928; Zimmermann, 1921a, Stoelting, 1921). From left to right: Dynamometer by Collin, Sternberg, and Ulmann - grip strength; Andrew's dynamometer – arms spreading force; Johnson's gnathodynamometer – bite pressure strength

Other Tools and Devices

Some of the tools and devices used in psychological laboratories had very specialized functions. As they could not be included in our categorization, we devoted a separate chapter exclusively to these instruments.

Illusion Shapes

Täuschungsfiguren (GE)

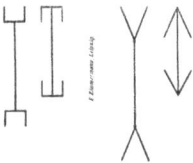

Figure 139. Illusion Shapes (Zimmermann, 1923a)

Metal models of Müller-Lyer figures are used for the examination of illusory perception in blind people (Patterson, 1972). Made of brass rods with a diameter of 5 mm and basic length of 20 cm, the figures are available in both fixed and telescopic variants. The inner part of the main rod in the telescopic variant is graduated so that the length of the extension can easily be determined. The models were equipped with knuckle joints which allow the models to be shaped into both figure versions: the arrows pointing inwards and outwards.

Wundt's Stroboscope for Accurate Psychological Studies

Stroboskop nach Wundt, für exakte psychologische Versuche (GE)

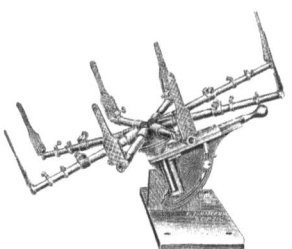

Figure 140. Wundt's Stroboscope for Accurate Psychological Studies (Zimmermann, 1903)

Wundt's stroboscope is a highly accurate instrument driven by an electric motor which enables presentation of eight subsequent images. The central part carries eight radial telescopic arms smoothly adjustable between the lengths of 21 and 51 cm. Paper cards with images are attached at the ends of these arms, facing inwards, to the center of the circle. Fixation is provided by a couple of flat springs. The plate on which the device is mounted can be fastened to the edge of a table by clamps, which also allows setting the device's rotation axis to any position between 0 to 90°.

Area Estimator[36]

Flächenschätzer (GE)

Figure 141. Area Estimator (Zimmermann, 1928)

---

36   http://history.psu.cas.cz/machinery/area_estimator.html

 The function of the area estimator is to perform comparisons between the sizes of two rectangular areas. The test subject is required to set the area of one window according to the pre-set example. A black piece of strong metal sheet contains two identical rectangular openings (windows). At the back of the sheet, surrounding the two windows, there are sliding tracks for a couple of small metal plates. When moved, the plates reduce the maximum area of the rectangular windows. The plates are adjusted by micrometer screws whose heads protrude from the sides of the sheet. The scale at the back of the device shows the current width of the rectangle with 0.1 mm accuracy.

Lehmann's Apparatus for the Accurate Testing of the Ability to Make Eye Estimations of Distance[37]

Apparat zur Genauigkeitsprüfung des Augenmasses nach Lehmann (GE)

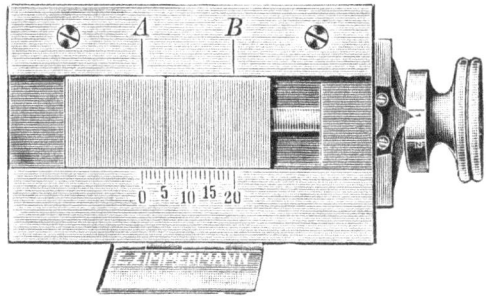

Figure 142. *Lehmann's Apparatus for the Accurate Testing of the Ability to Make Eye Estimations of Distance (Zimmermann, 1923a)*

 The turning of a micrometer screw moves a slider with a thin vertical line along a sliding track. The test subject is asked to position this line between two marks (*A* and *B*) drawn on the device's body above the slider. The instruction may vary between positioning the line exactly in the middle and dividing the segment in a particular ratio, e.g. 1:4, 19:1, etc. As soon as the test subject reports having finished the task, the experimenter uncovers the hidden scale in the lower part to check the actual value. To make the measurement more precise, the head of the micrometer screw is also graduated. One turn of the screw shifts the slider by 0.5 mm. Maximum accuracy of the measurement is 0.1 mm.

---

37   http://history.psu.cas.cz/machinery/lehmann_accurate_testing.html

Two Deceptive Weights

Zwei Täuschungsgewichte (GE)

Figure 143. Two Deceptive Weights (Zimmermann, 1928)

The two weights showed on left side of Figure 143 made of wood and both contain a cavity for the insertion of other weights made of lead. The weight of the weights can be modified according to the experimental requirements, while maintaining identical visual appearance.

The two lead weights on the right side of the Figure 143 differ in size but they both weigh 200 g. The larger one is hollow, and when the top is unscrewed, it can be filled with finely crushed lead. This way, the weight ratio between the two weights can be changed.

Three Deceptive Weights Designed by Claparède

Drei Täuschungsgewichte nach Claparède (GE)

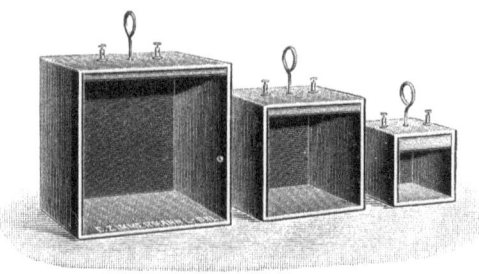

Figure 144. Three Deceptive Weights Designed by Claparède (Zimmermann, 1928)

The set is comprised of three wooden boxes of different sizes with the back side uncovered. Despite the size differences, all three boxes equally weigh 1.1 kg (Zimmermann, 1928). Experimental conditions can be modified by filling the cavity with additional weights. A specific point about this set is that the boxes contain inbuilt electric contacts: As soon as the weight is lifted by its handle, an electric circuit is closed and a connected device (e.g. timing device) is turned on.

Auxiliary Devices

The early psychological laboratories housed many tools that could not be considered as independent instruments, but were nevertheless essential for setting up even the most basic experiments. These auxiliary devices included various types of stands, mounts, switches, engines, and batteries.

Switches

Pohl's 'seesaw' Switch

Pohl'sche Wippe (GE)

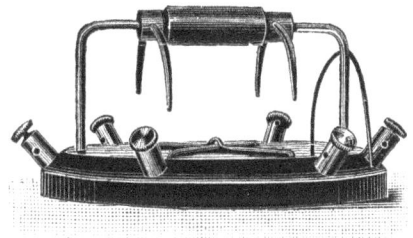

Figure 145. Pohl's Switch (Zimmermann, 1903)

This tool provides fast manual switching of the direction of the electric current flow. The battery poles are attached to contacts on the opposite sides of the switch. The current is then conducted to the cradles. The prongs of the first cradle are connected to the minus pole, whereas the prongs of the other cradle are connected to the plus pole. The non-conductive handle between the cradles is made of wood. The switch is also equipped with two pairs of diagonally connected contacts with mercury cups. The output wires must be connected to the contacts from both pairs to obtain an opposite polarity. The actual polarity is set by turning the handle and dipping one prong from each cradle into the mercury cups located on the base. The switch was originally used to provide fast change of current flow direction in physiological experiments involving muscle stimulation.

Du Bois-Reymond's Switch

Schlüssel nach Du Bois-Reymond (GE)

Figure 146. Du Bois-Reymond's Switch (Spindler & Hoyer, 1908)

This type of switch was already used in the first half of the nineteen century, as documented by Du Bois-Reymond's (1845 – 1849) laboratory diary. The principle of the switch is simple: Reclining of the handle connects its contact with a conductive surface and closes the electric circuit. The switch exists in a metal-mercury or metal-metal version.

Response Curve Measuring Devices

Graphical recordings of experimental data were highly analogous, which is why there were many devices whose function was to make the process of data analysis easier and more efficient.

Glass Gauge

Glasmassstäbe (GE)

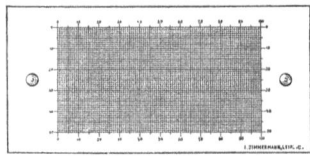

Figure 147. Glass Gauge (Zimmermann, 1912)

The glass gauge is a simple, yet useful tool. Basically, it is a millimeter grid drawn on a glass plate. When the plate is placed over a graphical recording, numerical values can be obtained. The gauge must always be placed over the recording with scale lines facing down to avoid the parallax error of measurement.

Von Frey's Curve Measuring Table

Kurven-Messtisch nach von Frey (GE)

Figure 148. Von Frey's Curve Measuring Table (Zimmermann, 1903)

Von Frey's table makes the analysis of obtained graphical recordings even more efficient. The analyzed section of the recording is fastened to the table desk. The mechanism of reading the recording consists in moving the table desk (in both directions) against a static mark using micrometric screws. The values are obtained from the circular scales on the corresponding screws. The solid construction of the table enables mounting of a microscope with a crosshair to enhance the accuracy of measurement. The micrometric screws are graduated in hundredths of millimeters.

Scripture's Curve Measuring Table

Kurvenmesstisch nach Scripture (GE)

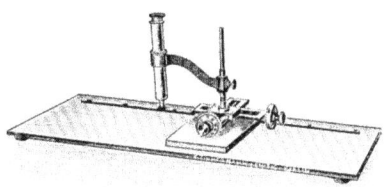

Figure 149. Scripture's Curve Measuring Table (Zimmermann, 1928)

In contrast to Von Frey's table, this tool allows the analysis of considerably larger graphical recordings. Instead of a moving the desk with the recording spread over it, Scripture's table has an inbuilt microscope which moves over a statically fixed recording. The actual distance between two points on the recording is obtained by subtracting the values of the starting and end positions on the scale with accuracy of 0.01 millimeter. A similar design is employed in Jacquet's analyzer of tracing.

Straub's Curve Projector

Kurvenkino nach prof. Straub (GE)

Figure 150. Straub's Curve Projector (Jaquet, n.d.)

The projector of Professor Straub is especially suitable for demonstrations of graphical recordings in front of a wide audience; alternatively, it proved to be useful in the analysis of curves with very small amplitudes. The device is equipped with an arc carbon lamp which emits very bright and intense white light. A holder with a glass diapositive (a recording inscribed into the carbon black spread over a sheet of glass) moves on a prismatic rail to adjust the focus. The prismatic rail also carried an optical system which regulates the size of the projection and tunes up the sharpness of the image.

Batteries and Accumulators

Researchers in early laboratories used many different types of batteries, capacitive cells, and accumulators. Zimmermann's catalogue (1923f) offers 7 types of power cells and 3 variants of accumulators. In this chapter we present descriptions of the most commonly used power sources.

Lead Accumulator

Bleiakkumulator (GE)

Figure 151. Lead Accumulator (Zimmermann, n.d.)

Lead accumulator battery advertised in Zimmermann's catalogue (1923f, list 46) consists of 4 cells, providing an 8 V voltage and nominal power of 3.6 Ah. It is intended mainly for powering electromotors.

Meidinger's Power Cell

Meidinger-Element (GE)

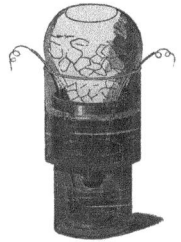

Figure 152. Meidinger's Power Cell (Zimmermann, 1903)

Meidinger's cell is based on the principle of a double-solution cell (solutions of blue vitriol and white vitriol) and a combination of two metals – zinc and copper (Nechvátal, 1920). Meidinger's cells were used by Wundt (1909) as stable sources of direct current.

Copper Element Cell

Cupron-Element (GE)

Figure 153. Copper Element Cell (Zimmermann, 1928)

This power cell uses cupric sulfate to generate electric current. It provides a 0.8 V output voltage. The cell is designed so that it does not require any maintenance and it does not produce any poisonous gases during operation.

Transmissions, Engines and Tachometers

Transmissions connect the propelling devices with the instruments being propelled, allowing the user to control the application of the power. Early laboratories were often equipped with a central shaft driven by a single engine. The shaft offered several different settings with a set of wheels of various sizes providing different speeds. The rotational speed was transmitted to instruments by means of leather belts. When the laboratory had no central shaft, the individual instrument sets had to be driven by engines and the rotation power had to be adjusted by table transmissions (see Figure 154).

Figure 154. Table Transmission (Zimmermann, 1903). The depicted transmission provides transmission ratio up to 1:7.5.

Tachometers are particularly useful when successful replication of an experimental procedure depends on achieving an exact propelling speed, like in the experiments with color mixing devices. Tachometers are attached to the central axis of the tested shaft to measure the number of revolutions in a defined time interval. Due to its contact nature, the measurement itself decreases the rotation speed of the shaft. To keep the measurement process equivalent, it is necessary to use the same type of tachometer in the intended replication.

In most cases, instrumental equipment was propelled manually or by electric motors. Early electric motors were either powered by direct current generated by batteries, or drew power from central distribution. More recently, engines powered by alternating current were applied. Power of the engines was specified in horse power units and later also in watts. The engineers designing electric motors were confronted with the issue of controlling the speed of revolutions. For example, Helmholtz's electromagnetically controlled rotation apparatus used a device called centrifugal regulator, in which centrifugal force pushes the contact out of the middle against a spring. The pressure force of the spring is regulated by a graduated micrometric screw. When the rotation speed exceeds the limit set by the screw, the contact is broken and the motor is switched off. When the motor is not working, the rotation speed decreases and the contact is closed again. The achievement of a constant rotation speed is indicated by a regular tapping sound of the regulator (Titchener, 1895).

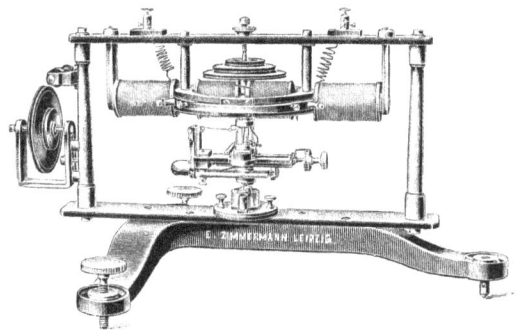

Figure 155. Helmholtz's Electromagnetically Controlled Rotation Apparatus (Zimmermann, 1903)

Electricity was not the only energy source used for powering engines. An interesting example of an alternative source is provided by the water-power engine. Principally, it is a small turbine connected to water mains. The turbine's rotation speed is regulated by the volumetric flow rate of the water passing through the mains. This type of engine provides considerably more power than electric motors powered by batteries do, which is why it can be successfully used with instruments highly demanding in terms of energy, such as Wundt's chronograph (Titchener, 1895).

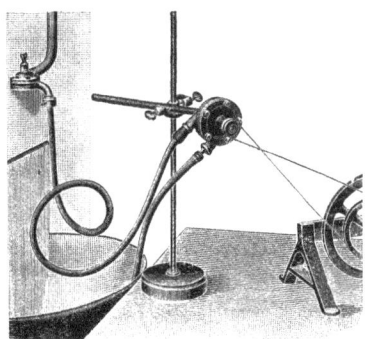

Figure 156. Water-Power Engine (Spindler & Hoyer, 1908)

Conclusion

At this point we have approached the very end of our journey through the historical laboratories of experimental psychology. The instruments chosen for this book represent some of the most typical instances of equipment used in those days. By cataloguing, precise identification and, in some cases, rediscovery of forgotten functions of the historical instruments we attempted to provide a tool which could increase the understanding of the knowledge base created by the founders of experimental psychology. We hope that our work will make study of primary sources easier for other researchers, who will find scientific literature featuring instruments and mechanisms described in this book more comprehensible.

The period addressed in the book covered approximately the years between 1870 and 1930. After 1930, a major boom of electronics almost instantly rendered the previously widely used pneumatic, mechanical or electromechanical systems obsolete. Laboratories and universities quickly started to dispose of their "outmoded" brass, wooden and steel apparatus, replacing it with modern electronic alternatives. Two great wars also took their toll on the past heritage, and as a result, very little of the original laboratory equipment has survived until this day. For that reason, we should feel even more encouraged to study it closely and preserve it for the future generations.

Summary

Psychological machinery: Experimental devices in early psychological laboratories covers the topic of experimental instrumentation at the turn of the 20th century. The book introduces the role of instruments in the process of establishing psychological science. Attention is paid to issues of identifying historical devices and problems with rediscovering their functionality.

The authors focus on identification and classification of most relevant instrumental equipment. The core of the book consists of categorized list of instruments with detailed description of their purpose and mechanical design. The categorization covers recording and time measuring devices, instruments designated for the research of human senses, memory, and learning, and devices for physiological measurement. The publication also includes a companion website with short videos demonstrating the operation of selected instruments.

Bibliography

Arnold, F. (1858). *Die physiologische Anstalt der Universität Heidelberg von 1853 bis 1858* [Physiological Institute of the University of Heidelberg from 1853 to 1858]. Heidelberg: Akademische Verlags-Buchhandlung von J. C. B. Mohr.

Bailey, E. H. S., Nichols, L. (1888). The sense of taste. *Science*, 9, 145–146.

Benjamin, L. T. Jr. (1997). *A history of psychology: original sources and contemporary research* (2nd ed.). New York: McGraw-Hill Companies, Inc.

Berliner, B. (1907). Der Anstieg der reinen Farbenerregung im Sehorgan. [The increase of pure color stimulation in the eye]. *Psychologische Studien*, 3, 91–155.

Bjork, D. W. (1983). *The compromised scientist: William James in development of American psychology*. New York: Columbia University Press.

Boring, E. G. (1942). *Sensation and perception in the history of experimental psychology*. New York: Appleton-Century-Crofts.

Boring, E. G. (1950). *A history of experimental psychology* (2nd ed.). New York: Appleton-Century-Crofts.

Cattell, J. McK. (1886a). Über die Trägheit der Netzhaut und des Sehcentrums [The inertia of retina and visual cortex]. *Philosophische Studien*, 3, 94–127.

Cattell, J. McK. (1886b). The time taken up by cerebral operations. *Mind*, 11, 377–392.

Cattell, J. McK. (1888). The psychological laboratory at Leipsic. *Mind*, 13, 37–51.

Cattell, J. McK. (1928). Early psychological laboratories. *Science*, 67, 543–548.

Chmelař, V. (1935). Vývoj trvání aktivní optické pozornosti dětí 6–11 letých [Development of duration of active optical attention in children 6–11 years]. *Psychologie*, 1, 28–35.

Cyon, E. (1876a). *Atlas zur Methodik der physiologischen Experimente und Vivisectionen: LIV Tafeln in Holzschnitt* [Atlas on the methodology of physiological experiments and vivisection: LIV panels in woodcut]. Giessen: J. Ricker'sche Buchhandlung.

Cyon, E. (1876b). *Methodik der physiologischen Experimente und Vivisectionen* [Methodology of physiological experiments and vivisection]. Giessen: J. Ricker'sche Buchhandlung.

Diehl, J. A., McKeever, W. F. (1987). Absence of exposure time influence on late-ralized face recognition and object naming latency tasks. *Brain and Cognition*, 3, 347–359.

Dodge, R. (1907). An improved exposure apparatus. *Psychological Bulletin*, 4, 10–13.

DONDERS, F. C. (1868). Die Schnelligkeit psychischer Prozesse [The speed of mental processes]. *Archiv für Anatomie und Physiologie und wissenschaftliche Medizin*, 657–681.
DOVE, H. W. (1841). Die Combination der Eindrücke beider Ohren und beider Augen zu einem Eindruck [The combination of perceptions from both ears and both eyes to a single perception]. *Monatsberichte der Berliner preussische Akademie der Wissenschaften*, 41, 251–252.
DRAAISMA, D. (Ed.) (1992). Een laboratorium voor de ziel, Gerard Heymans en het begin van de experimentele psychologie [A laboratory for the soul, Gerard Heymans and the beginning of experimental psychology]. Groningen: Universiteitsmuseum.
DU BOIS-REYMOND, E. (1845–1849). *H. VII, Experiments 26. 2. 45–49*. Laboratory diary. Staatsbibliothek zu Berlin, Preußischer Kulturbesitz: Handschriftenabteilung / Sammlung Darmstaedter. Retrieved from http://vlp.mpiwg-berlin.mpg.de/references?id=lit16333&page=a0001
FELDMANN, H. (1995). The Galton whistle and discovery of presbycusis. Images from the history of otorhinolaryngology, exemplified by equipment from the collection of the Ingolstadt German Medical History Museum. *Laryngorhinootologie*, 74, 329–334.
FRIEDRICH, M. (1883). Über die Apperceptionsdauer bei einfachen und zusammengesetzten Vorstellungen [On the duration of apperception for simple and complex ideas]. *Philosophische Studien*, 1, 39–77.
GIESE, F. (1925). *Handbuch psychotechnischer Eignungsprüfungen* [The handbook of psycho-technical performance testing]. Halle a. d. S.: Carl Marhold Verlagsbuchhandlung.
GUNDLACH, H. (1983). *Faksimilenachdruck: E. Zimmermann, Preis-Liste XVII* [Reprint: E. Zimmermann, Price-list XVII]. Passau: Universität Passau.
HAHN, K. (1964). *Technika psychologickej inštrumentalizácie* [Engineering of psychological instrumentation]. Bratislava: SPN.
HARPER, R. S. (1950). The first psychological laboratory. *Isis*, 41, 158–161.
HELMHOLTZ, H. VON (1870). *Die Lehre von den Tonempfindungen als physiologische Grundlage für die Theorie der Musik* [On the sensations of tone as a physiological basis for the theory of music]. Braunschweig: Vieweg.
HOSKOVEC, J., NAKONEČNÝ, M., SEDLÁKOVÁ, M. (2003). *Psychologie XX. století: některé významné směry a školy* [Psychology of the XX. century, some significant trends and schools]. Praha: Karolinum.
JAQUET, J. (n.d.) *Jaquet Apparatus: Catalogue 503*. Basel. Retrieved from http://vlp.mpiwg-berlin.mpg.de/library/data/lit13643
KLEIN, F. (1977). *Deutschland von 1897/98 bis 1917* [Germany from 1897/98 to 1917]. Berlin: VEB Deutscher Verlag der Wissenschaften.

KNOTT, L. E. (1921). *L. E. Knott Apparatus Company: Scientific Instruments, Catalogue 26.* Boston.

KROHN, W. O. (1892). Facilities in experimental psychology at the various German universities. *American Journal of Psychology*, 4, 585–94.

LANC, O. (1966). *Základy přístrojové techniky experimentální psychologie* [The basics of instrumental equipment in experimental psychology]. Praha: Univerzita Karlova.

LANGENDORFF, O. (1891). *Physiologische Graphik* [Physiological graphics]. Leipzig und Wien: Franz Deuticke.

LIFKA, B. (1923). Dastichovy zápisky z prvé cesty po Německu 1865 [Dastich's notes from his first trip to Germany 1865]. *Česká mysl*, 19, 35–42.

MARX, M. (1913). *Apparate für psychologische Untersuchungen, Preisliste Nr. 5.* [Apparatus for psychological research, Price-list No. 5], Berlin.

MÜNSTERBERG, H. (1893). *Psychological laboratory of Harvard University.* Retreived from http://psychclassics.yorku.ca/Munster/Lab/.

NECHVÁTAL, T. (1920). *Telegrafní, telefonní, návěštní a zabezpečovací zařízení u státních drah* [Telegraph, telephone, signal, and safety devices by national railway system]. Praha: Šolc a Šimáček.

OTTO, J. (1898). *Ottův slovník naučný* [Otto's encyclopedic dictionary] (Volume 13, entry Cardiograph). Praha: J. Otto.

OTTO, J. (1900). *Ottův slovník naučný* [Otto's encyclopedic dictionary] (Volume 16, entry Leipzig, p. 83). Praha: J. Otto.

PATTERSON, J., KENNETH, D. (1972). Haptic perception of the Mueller-Lyer illusion by the blind. *Perceptual and Motor Skills*, 35, 819–824.

PERERA, T. B., HAUPT, E. J. (2000). *Museum of the history of reaction time research.* Retreived from http://tomperera.com/psychology_museum/mrt.htm

PISKO, F. J. (1865). *Die neueren Apparate der Akustik. Für Freunde der Naturwissenschaft und der Tonkunst* [The modern apparatus in acoustics. For the friends of the science and the art of music]. Wien: Druck und Verlag von Carl Gerold's Sohn.

RAMEŠ, M. (1928). Nový psychologický přístroj – precizoskop [The new psychological instrument – precisescope]. *Česká mysl*, 24, 17–23.

ROTHE, R. (1893). *Spezialitäten physiologischer Apparate* [Specialized physiological apparatus]. Prague: Hofbuchdruckerei A. Haase.

SCHMIDGEN, H., EVANS, R. B. (2003). The virtual laboratory: A new on-line resource for the history of psychology. *History of Psychology*, 2, 208–213.

SCHRAVEN, T. (2004). *The Hipp Chronoscope.* The Virtual Laboratory (ISSN 1866–4784). Retrieved from http://vlp.mpiwg-berlin.mpg.de/references?id=enc13&page=p0005

SPERLING, G. (1960). The information available in brief visual presentations. *Psy-*

chological Monographs: General and Applied, 11, 1–29.

SPINDLER & HOYER (1908). *Apparate für psychologische Untersuchungen, Preisliste XXI* [Apparatus for psychological research, Price-list XXI]. Göttingen.

SPINDLER & HOYER (1921). *Apparate für psychologische Untersuchungen, Katalog XXI* [Apparatus for psychological research, Catalogue XXI]. Göttingen.

STOELTING, C. H. (1930). *Apparatus, tests and supplies for psychology, psychometry, psychotechnology, psychiatry, neurology, anthropology, phonetics, physiology, and pharmacology.* Chicago: C. H. Stoelting, Co.

TITCHENER, E. B. (1895). *Photograph album on psychological instruments.* Unpublished private catalogue of instruments and devices. Retrieved from http://vlp.mpiwg-berlin.mpg.de/library/data/lit13651.

TITCHENER, E. B. (1905). *Experimental psychology: A manual of laboratory practice, Vol. II: Quantitative experiments, part 1: Student's manual.* New York, London: Macmillan and Co.

VOBOŘIL, D., JELÍNEK, M., KVĚTON, P. (in press). Experimental evaluation of tachistoscopic measurement: A step beyond Wundt's criticism. *American Journal of Psychology.*

VOLKMANN, A. W. (1859). Das Tachistoskop, ein Instrument, welches bei Untersuchung des momentanen Sehens den Gebrauch des elektrischen Funkens ersetzt [The tachistoscope, an instrument that can replace electric spark in research of momentary vision]. *Berichte über die Verhandlungen der Königlich Sächsischen Gesellschaft der Wissenschaften zu Leipzig: Mathematisch-Physische Classe*, 11, 90–98.

WHIPPLE, G. M. (1901a). An analytic study of the memory image and the process of judgment in the discrimination of clangs and tones. *American Journal of Psychology*, 12, 409–457.

WHIPPLE, G. M. (1901b). An analytic study of the memory image and the process of judgment in the discrimination of clangs and tones. *American Journal of Psychology*, 13, 219–268.

WOODWORTH, R. S., SCHLOSBERG, H. (1959). *Experimentálna psychológia* [Experimental psychology]. Bratislava: Vydavateľstvo slovenskej akadémie vied.

WUNDT, W. (1893a). Chronograph und Chronoskop: Notiz zu einer Bemerkung J. M. Cattell's [Chronograph and chronoscope: A note to the J. M. Cattell's comments]. *Philosophische Studien*, 8, 653–654.

WUNDT, W. (1893b). *Grundzüge der physiologischen Psychologie* [Principles of physiological psychology] (4th ed.). Leipzig: Engelmann.

WUNDT, W. (1900). Zur Kritik tachistoskopischer Versuche [On critique of tachistoscope experiments]. *Philosophische Studien*, 15, 287–317.

WUNDT, W. (1909). Das Institut für experimentelle Psychologie [The institute for experimental psychology]. In Rektor und Senat der Universität Leipzig (Eds.),

Festschrift zur Feier des 500 jährigen Bestehens der Universität Leipzig (pp. 118-133). Leipzig: S. Hirzel.

WUNDT, W. (1920). *Erlebtes und Erkanntes* [Experiences and findings]. Stuttgart: Alfred Kröner Verlag.

ZIMMERMANN, E. (1895a). *Liste XI, 1895: Neuer Rotationsapparat nach Dr. Marbe* [Catalogue XI, 1895: The new rotation apparatus by Dr. Marbe]. Leipzig.

ZIMMERMANN, E. (1895b). *Liste XII, September 1895: Sphygmograph nach Prof. v. Frey* [Catalogue XII, September 1895: Sphygmograph by Prof. v. Frey]. Leipzig.

ZIMMERMANN, E. (1896). *Liste XIII, August 1896: Rotationsapparat für Farbscheiben* [Catalogue XIII, August 1896: Rotation apparatuses for color mixing]. Leipzig.

ZIMMERMANN, E. (1900). *Psychologische und physiologische Apparate, Mikrotome* [Psychological and physiological apparatuses, microtome]. Leipzig: Fr. Richter.

ZIMMERMANN, E. (1902). *Juni 1902: Neuer vereinfachter Registrier-Apparat (Kymographion)* [June 1902: The new simplified registration device (Kymograph)]. Leipzig: Hallberg & Büchting.

ZIMMERMANN, E. (1903). *XVIII Preis-Liste über psychologische und physiologische apparate* [XVIII Price-list of the psychological and physiological apparatus]. Leipzig.

ZIMMERMANN, E. (1904). *Apparate zu experimental-psychologischen Untersuchungen nach Angaben des Herrn Prof. Dr. Sommer* [Apparatuses for experimental psychological research designed by Dr. Sommer]. Leipzig.

ZIMMERMANN, E. (1905). *Kehlton-Schreiber nach F. Krueger und W. Wirth* [Kehlton-writer by F. Krueger and W. Wirth]. Leipzig.

ZIMMERMANN, E. (1912). *Liste 25: Psychologische und Physiologische Apparate* [Catalogue 25: Psychological and physiological apparatuses]. Leipzig, Berlin.

ZIMMERMANN, E. (1921a). *Liste 37: Über Registrier-Apparate und Zubehör* [Catalogue 37: On registration devices and accessories]. Leipzig, Berlin.

ZIMMERMANN, E. (1921b). *Liste 42: Über Registrier-Apparate und Zubehör* [Catalogue 42: On registration devices and accessories]. Leipzig, Berlin.

ZIMMERMANN, E. (1922a). *Liste 34: Über Optik, Ophthalmologische Apparate* [Catalogue 34: On optics, ophthalmic apparatuses]. Leipzig, Berlin.

ZIMMERMANN, E. (1922b). *Liste 40: Über akustische und phonetische Instrumente* [Catalogue 40: On acoustic and phonetic instruments]. Leipzig, Berlin.

ZIMMERMANN, E. (1922c). *Liste 41: Über Unterbrecher, Zeitschreiber, Induktorien* [Catalogue 41: On interrupters, time recorders, inductors]. Leipzig, Berlin.

ZIMMERMANN, E. (1923a). *Liste 33: Über Psychotechnik* [Catalogue 33: On psychotechnique]. Leipzig, Berlin.

ZIMMERMANN, E. (1923b). *Liste 35: Über Tachistoskope, Gedächtnisapparate* [Catalogue 35: On tachistoscopes, memory devices]. Leipzig, Berlin.
ZIMMERMANN, E. (1923c). *Liste 36: Über Apparate für Anthropometrie, Sinnesempfindungen und Sinnestäuschungen* [Catalogue 36: On apparatus for anthropometry, sensory perception, and sensory illusion]. Leipzig, Berlin.
ZIMMERMANN, E. (1923d). *Liste 38: Über Zeitmeßinstrumente, Kontrollapparate* [Catalogue 38: On time measuring devices, control apparatuses]. Leipzig, Berlin.
ZIMMERMANN, E. (1923e). *Liste 39: Über Reaktions-Taster, Stromkreisutensilien* [Catalogue 39: On reaction keys, electro equipment]. Leipzig, Berlin.
ZIMMERMANN, E. (1923f). *Liste 46: Über Stative, Motore, Meßinstrumente Zubehör.* [Catalogue 46: On stands, motors, measuring instruments accessories]. Leipzig, Berlin.
ZIMMERMANN, E. (1928). *Liste 50: Psychologische und Physiologische Apparate.* [Catalogue 50: Psychological and physiological apparatuses]. Leipzig, Berlin.
ZIMMERMANN, E. (n.d.). *Psychologische-Pädagogische Psychotechnische Apparate Liste 51. Physiologische Apparate Liste 200. Mikrotome nach Minot Liste 203* [Psychological-pedagogical psychotechnical apparatuses catalogue 51. Physiological apparatuses Catalogue 200. Microtome by Minot catalogue 203]. Leipzig, Berlin. Retrieved from http://vlp.mpiwg-berlin.mpg.de/library/data/lit24230
ZUCKERMAN, M. (1955). The effect of frustration on the perception of neutral and aggressive words. *Journal of Personality*, 4, 407–422.

Instrument Index

Air Compressor	88
Area Estimator	110
Aubert's Variable Rotating Sector	62
Bellows	89
Bernstein's Spring (Cyclic) Interrupter	26
Bert's Stethograph	99
Bert-Style Cycle Stethograph	100
Bottle Organ	86
Bowditch-Baltzar's Contact Clock	24
Cardiograph According to Burdon-Sanderson	96
Cattell's Acoustic Switch	32
Colored Disc Rotated by Clockwork	58
Colored Disc Rotated by Electric Motor	59
Color Variator (Original Construction)	60
Consumable Material	61
Contact Pendulum	22
Contact Pole Clock	25
Copper Element Cell	117
Dodge's Mirror Tachistoscope	69
Double Magnet Marker	52
Drop Phonometer	80
Du Bois-Reymond's Switch	114
Dubois' Ergograph	107
Dynamometers	108
Ebbinghaus' Aesthesiometer	76
Electromagnetic Sound Hammer	83
Electromagnetic Tuning Fork	34
Electromagnetic Tuning Fork (for direct time measurement)	37
Electromagnetic Tuning Fork with Resonance Tube	35
Electromagnetic Tuning Fork with Mercury Contact	35
Electropneumatic Converter	55
Fixation Apparatus	47
Förster's Perimeter	71
Galton Whistle	85
Glass Gauge	114
Gutzmann's Tuning Fork Apparatus	36
Hand Driven Colored Disc	57
Hardy's Self Recording Perimeter	72
Helmholtz's Color Mixing Apparatus	56
Helmholtz's Electromagnetically Controlled Rotation Apparatus	119
Hering's Optical Color Mixing Apparatus	56
Hipp's Drop Apparatus	17
Hipp's Chronoscope	16
Hornbostel's Travelling Tonometer	84
Illusion Shapes	109
Jaquet's Graphic Chronometer	18

INSTRUMENT INDEX

Klemensiewicz's Air Pressure Transmission Chronograph 23
Klemm's Hand Tachistoscope 68
Kymograph with Endless Paper 40
Lamp-Blacking Frame According to von Frey 45
Lamp-Blacking Frame for Hering Loops 46
Large Falling Hammer Delay Timer 21
Large Weight-Driven Kymograph 44
Lead Accumulator 116
Lehmann's Apparatus for the Accurate Testing of the Ability to Make Eye Estimations of Distance 111
Lehmann's Pneumograph 98
Lehmann-Style Plethysmograph 100
Lip Key 32
Ludwig–Baltzar's Kymograph 38
Ludwig-Cyon's Mercury Manometer 102
Marbe's Rotator 59
Marey's Chronograph 54
Marey's Pneumograph 98
Marey's Tambour 48
Marey-Style Transmitted Sphygmograph 103
Meidinger's Power Cell 117
Memory Association Device 94
Metronome with Electrical Interrupting Device 23
Meumann-Style Ergograph 108
Meumann's Universal Contact Apparatus 27
Mischotte's Sevenfold Colored Disc 58
Moede's Tremometer 105
Mosso's Ergograph 106
Müller's Episcotister 62
Netschajeff's Tachistoscope 66
Netschajeff's Tachistoscope, Giese's Construction 66
Ophtalmotrope (Model of the Muscles of the Eye) 73
Piston Registering Apparatus 50
Pohl's 'seesaw' Switch 113
Politzer's Acoumeter 81
Ranschburg's Apparatus for Testing Perception, Association, and Memory (Mnemometer) 93
Reaction Switch with Platinum Contact and Air Capsule 30
Recording Apparatus for Pulse etc 104
Recording Drum on Stand 45
Registering Capsule for Marey's Cardiograph 96
Resonators 89
Römer's Acoustic Switch: Apparatus for Acoustic Stimulation and Response 31
Rotary Apparatus for Memory Testing Designed by Müller-Pilzecker 92
Rotary Tachistoscope 65
Rotator with Split Shaft (Counter-Rotating Discs) 61
Sanderson's Cardiograph 97
Scripture's Curve Measuring Table 115
School Kymograph (with Clockwork and Friction Gearing) 39
Schumann's Chronograph 20
Signal Marker Pen according to Pfeil 53

Simple Contact Clock 24
Simple Reaction Key 28
Simple Reaction Key by Zimmermann... 29
Simple Tuning Fork 33
Sommer's Apparatus for Analyzing the Motions of the Hand in Three Dimensions 106
Sound Pendulums... 82
Spearman's Aesthesiometer 76
Spectrometric Apparatus.. 74
Stern Tone Variator 87
Stratton-Style Balance for Pressure (Wundt's Aerometer) 79
Straub's Curve Projector..116
Table Transmission 118
Tachistoscope with Camera-Like Mechanical Shutter 68
Taste Stimulators.. 91
Telegraph Key (American Model).. 29
Ten-fold Finger Reaction Apparatus with Stopper Contacts 30
Three Deceptive Weights Designed by Claparède...112
Tone Box.. 85
Tube Pneumograph 99
Two Deceptive Weights 112
Universal Kymograph.. 41
Universal Marking Lever... 51
Vertical Marking Apparatus 51
Vibrating Pen 53
Von Frey's Apparatus for Measuring Threshold Value of Pressure Sensitivity............................. 78
Von Frey's Curve Measuring Table 115
Von Frey's Electromagnetic Stimulating Lever... 77
Von Frey's Hair Aesthesiometer 75
Von Frey's Optical Bench 74
Von Frey's Tonograph 101
Von Frey-Style Sphygmograph.. 103
Von Frey-Style Temperature Point... 75
Water-Power Engine 119
Wavograph According to Fick 50
Wirth's and Berliner's Pendulum Tachistoscope 67
Wirth's Memory Apparatus.. 94
Wooden Whistle... 84
Writing Utensils for Registrations 54
Wundt's Demonstration Aesthesiometer 78
Wundt's Chronograph 19
Wundt's Kymograph.. 43
Wundt's Ophtalmotrope for Demonstrating the Actions of the Muscles of the Eyeball 73
Wundt's Perimeter.. 70
Wundt's Sound Interruptor... 90
Wundt's Stroboscope for Accurate Psychological Studies 110
Wundt's Tachistoscope... 64
Wundt's Timing Apparatus 25
Zoth's Instrument for Testing Acutement of Hearing 81
Zwaardemaker's Instrument for Testing Sense of Smell (Olfactometer) 90

www.ingramcontent.com/pod-product-compliance
Ingram Content Group UK Ltd.
Pitfield, Milton Keynes, MK11 3LW, UK
UKHW021836210426
5322IPUK00021B/321